Winnetka-Northfield Public Library

3 1240 00549 6109

JUN   - 2016

D1286959

Withdrawn

WINNETKA-NORTHFIELD
PUBLIC LIBRARY DISTRICT
WINNETKA, IL 60093
847-446-7220

LESSONS IN
THE ART OF WAR

DEDICATION

To Patrick Gallegos,
martial artist, training partner, and friend

LESSONS IN
THE ART OF WAR

MARTIAL STRATEGIES *for the* SUCCESSFUL FIGHTER

Martina Sprague

TUTTLE Publishing

Tokyo | Rutland, Vermont | Singapore

Please note that the publisher and author of this book are NOT RESPONSIBLE in any manner whatsoever for any injury that may result from practicing the techniques and/or following the instructions given within. Martial arts training can be dangerous—both to you and to others—if not practiced safely. If you're in doubt as to how to proceed or whether your practice is safe, consult with a trained martial arts teacher before beginning. Since the physical activities described herein may be too strenuous in nature for some readers, it is also essential that a physician be consulted prior to training.

Published by Tuttle Publishing, an imprint of Periplus Editions (HK) Ltd.

www.tuttlepublishing.com

Copyright © 2011 Martina Sprague

All rights reserved. No part of this publication may be reproduced or utilized in any form or by any means, electronic or mechanical, including photocopying, recording, or by any information storage and retrieval system, without prior written permission from the publisher.

Library of Congress Cataloging-in-Publication Data

Sprague, Martina.
  Lessons in the art of war : martial arts strategies from East and West / Martina Sprague. -- 1st ed.
      p. cm.
  Includes bibliographical references.
  ISBN 978-0-8048-4097-2 (hardcover)
1. Military art and science--Philosophy. 2. Sunzi, 6th cent. B.C. 3. Clausewitz, Carl von, 1780-1831. 4. Strategy. 5. East and West. 6. Martial arts--Philosophy. 7. Combat. 8. Military readiness. I. Title.
  U21.2.S67 2011
  355.02--dc22

                                        2010053840

ISBN 978-0-8048-4097-2

Distributed by

North America, Latin America & Europe
Tuttle Publishing
364 Innovation Drive
North Clarendon,
VT 05759-9436 U.S.A.
Tel: 1 (802) 773-8930; Fax: 1 (802) 773-6993
info@tuttlepublishing.com
www.tuttlepublishing.com

Japan
Tuttle Publishing
Yaekari Building, 3rd Floor
5-4-12 Osaki, Shinagawa-ku
Tokyo 141 0032
Tel: (81) 3 5437-0171; Fax: (81) 3 5437-0755
sales@tuttle.co.jp
www.tuttle.co.jp

Asia Pacific
Berkeley Books Pte. Ltd.
61 Tai Seng Avenue #02-12
Singapore 534167
Tel: (65) 6280-1330; Fax: (65) 6280-6290
inquiries@periplus.com.sg
www.periplus.com

First edition
14 13 12 11   10 9 8 7 6 5 4 3 2 1   1106TP

Printed in Singapore

TUTTLE PUBLISHING® is a registered trademark of Tuttle Publishing, a division of Periplus Editions (HK) Ltd.

CONTENTS

AN INTRODUCTION TO ASIAN AND WESTERN MILITARY THOUGHT

"Warfare is the greatest affair of state, the basis of life and death, the Way to survival or extinction."
— **Sun Tzu**

"War is the continuation of policy by other means. It is not only a political act, but also a true political instrument."
— **Carl von Clausewitz**

The martial arts have a long tradition emphasizing the wisdom of Asian philosophers, such as Sun Tzu[1] and Miyamoto Musashi, who owe much of their longevity to their use of universal principles for fighting. Sun Tzu, in the *Art of War* which might be the most widely studied of the Asian military treatises, did not speak of a mutually agreed upon code of conduct in battle but assessed the terrain, weather, and leadership to determine if the conditions favored military success. Although his battle philosophy emphasized quick victory, tactics of trickery and deception were elevated and described as virtues of great generals. Relatively little is known about Sun Tzu, but it is believed that he was a military strategist during China's turbulent Eastern Zhou Dynasty (c. 770-256 BCE). However, it is also possible that he was merely a writer who demonstrated an exceptionally pragmatic approach to warfare. According to some scholars, Sun Tzu's habit of prefacing many of his sayings with the phrase, "In ancient times," is an indication of the timeless nature of his ideas.[2]

The Japanese swordsman Miyamoto Musashi (c. 1584-c. 1645 CE), in *Book of Five Rings*, likewise viewed warfare as a pragmatic undertaking which purpose it was to defeat the enemy by killing him. A warrior taking up the sword to strike a fatal blow was expected to display an attitude of earnest intent.[3] Miyamoto Musashi followed a set of "natural" (scientific) principles and attributed his victories to proper understanding of these principles; one of which was the ability to stop an attack at the outset in order to stifle an opponent's speed and power (in sword fighting, for example, by blocking and redirecting the opponent's sword before the blow has fallen through the apex; in empty hand fighting, by jamming an opponent's kick at the chamber before his leg is fully extended).

The most prominent military thinker in the West was Carl von Clausewitz, an early nineteenth century Prussian soldier and strategist. Clausewitz presented his ideas as timeless and consistent theory of conflict. Like the Asian philosophers, he sought to uncover a universal nature of combat while illustrating his principles through the use of specific examples.[4] At the heart of his theory is the theme that combat is talked about in one way and exercised in another. He was foremost a practical soldier over a theoretician and had spent most of his life participating in warfare in one way or another. His varied career and experiences—he served in several positions including soldiering, staff officer, and educator of military personnel—and the fact that the national state in Prussia was militarized quickly and performed reasonably well in war, most certainly influenced his ideas. He was also affected by the Napoleonic Wars (c. 1803-1815 CE), where the constant aim seemed to be to occupy and subjugate the enemy country and destroy its armies. However, Clausewitz's ideas were not new. Three centuries earlier, Florentine statesman Niccolo Machiavelli had stressed that the aim of war was to achieve military superiority over other states, thereby avoiding becoming their victims. As a matter of survival, a state that waged war successfully could count on continued existence.

The purpose of this book is to compare and contrast Sun Tzu's and Carl von Clausewitz's theories of conflict and relate their findings to the development of the martial arts in the East and West. However, before embarking on a journey to discover how Asia's and Europe's historical views on tactics and strategy have affected the development of the combat arts, it is prudent to offer an overview (albeit a brief one) of the military histories of the respective regions and the origins of the ancient texts. China has a long dynastic history of rise and fall. China emphasized civilian supremacy over the military, and the highly bureaucratic state allowed the country to mobilize large resources for war. In early China (seventh century BCE), smaller states entered into defensive alliances against aggressive territorial states. In the Warring States period (453-221 BCE), these alliances collapsed as stronger states swallowed smaller states and grew even stronger. These larger states were able to raise armies numbering in the hundreds of thousands. Power was established and maintained through military means. Wars built states and dynasties, and warfare therefore proved necessary for the development of society. Military service provided an opportunity for upward social mobility, and professional armies replaced conscript armies according to military and social need.

The history of Asian military writings spans roughly 2,500 years. Not until the early twentieth century did Western texts come to dominate military thought. The classic texts of ancient China (the *Seven Military Classics of Ancient China*, including Sun Tzu's *Art of War*) are fundamental doctrines of tactics and strategy and demonstrate a preference for aggressive measures in war, often for the purpose of restoring the accepted social and political order.[5] Consider the harsh standards of discipline in the army as outlined in *Wei Liao-Tzu*: "If a drummer misses a beat he is executed."[6] Or according to *The Methods of the Ssu-Ma*: "What is the army's law regarding those who arrive after the appointed time?" The reply: "They should be decapitated!"[7] The underlying reason for this brutality was said to be the preservation of love and harmony among men. From an ethical viewpoint, if bringing peace to the people meant killing the enemy (or even one's own who failed to uphold the standards of military service), then killing was permissible.[8] In contrast to the Asian texts, Clausewitz held the view that "[g]rim severity and iron discipline may be able to preserve the military virtues of a unit, but it cannot create them."[9]

Chinese military theory was further stimulated by battlefield requirements and political and individual philosophies. Although historical accounts can be used as pillars of strength for building military theories, soldiers from different parts of the world have relied on a wide array of combat systems, and have exercised tactics and strategy in whichever way they have deemed the most appropriate for the particular geopolitical situation. China fought wars in order to overcome its enemies, but did not consider military force the only means by which the state could accomplish its goals. Many of the historical Chinese sources also stress the importance of ruling with moral authority. If the ruler did not maintain the social order, he would forfeit "Heaven's Mandate" and be considered unfit for holding authority through moral sanction.[10]

In contrast to the Western texts, which underscore the importance of aggressive action and scientific analysis, Asian philosophies further stress that studying, listening, and thinking are the keys to success. The long battlefield tradition of ancient China displays a strong relationship between the *wu* (military) and *wen* (civilian) spheres. Confucian philosophy promoted peace, yet military values shaped society's inclination for war. While the literati strove to elevate *wen*, warrior epics and tales often celebrated *wu* and spoke of the importance of combat and individual heroism. Analogies were frequently used to illustrate a point, as described in *T'ai Kung's Six Secret Teachings*, "If you grasp a knife but do not cut anything, you will lose the moment for profits. If you hold an ax but do not attack, then bandits will come."[11]

Sun Tzu's *Art of War* has proven particularly popular in the West because it appears to uncover the wisdom of the Asian philosophers, with focus on flexibility and deception rather than pitched battle and force. For example, contrast practitioners of the Chinese internal martial art of hsing-i chuan, who yield to the opponent's power and through a burst of energy use it against him, with Western wrestlers pitting strength against strength. Anecdotal stories and the paradoxical use of complementing opposites (yin and yang) further differentiate the Asian texts and martial arts from their Western counterparts.[12] They are attractive because they provide specific steps for every conceivable battlefield situation (for example, "On encircled terrain, I obstruct any openings"). Sun Tzu offered suggestions for fighting on narrow roads, in wild expanses, in forests, and in the darkness of night. The Chinese classics seem particularly fond of lists, as in the "ten fatal terrains," the "nine prohibitions," or the "five factors" from which victory can be drawn. Note that *The Methods of the Ssu-Ma* takes a slightly different tack by beginning many of its statements with "In general," thus leaving room for the variances of combat.

Although the Asian texts seem to offer a "cookbook" type approach to warfare through brief and precise statements, they are not meant to be read as "100 easy ways to win on the battlefield." Individual judgment is crucial to the successful application of the advice.[13] The fact that many of the historical sources have survived only in part, have not been translated, and contain popular story-telling and sectarian beliefs have complicated the Westerner's understanding of Asian warfare.[14] Furthermore, combat is neither simple nor simplistic; it is both scientific and artistic and requires the ability to grasp the essence of each unique situation.

Japan, including Okinawa where karate was used as a nonprofessional combat art, and Korea, faced different military and social environments than China. In Japan's forested and mountainous terrain large infantry armies proved inefficient. The common regional threats relating to robbers and bandits were resolved easier through specialized military elite forces. The samurai class developed from the need for court nobles to maintain order and ensure a continuous flow of resources from the countryside to the capital.[15] The samurai gained power in the provinces by assisting the state militarily and subduing rebellious uprisings. When the samurai were firmly established in the countryside, they developed their own networks which grew in size until the *shogunate*, a form of military government, was formed. It is debatable, however, whether or not service to the state was the primary goal of the samurai, as the strife to justify their continued existence even in times of peace is an indication of self-serving interests.

Korea was heavily influenced by the fighting arts of ancient China. However, it is worth noting that the tribal martial arts of Korea date to 2000-900 BCE.[16] From the sixth century CE, the state was provided with elite fighters through the Hwarang organization, which prepared young men for war by instructing them in military strategy and philosophy. These elite warriors lacked the political influence enjoyed by the Japanese samurai class.[17] There was also a growing need for the commoners to learn the combat arts. As late as the aftermath of the Korean War (1950-1953 CE), skill in taekwondo was viewed as a necessity for survival.[18]

The West likewise has a long battlefield tradition that can be traced to Classical Greece and Rome. The Greek historian Polybius expressed in the second century BCE that soldiers regarded "their one supreme duty not to flee or leave the ranks," and were "expected never to surrender or be captured."[19] Technology, innovation, discipline, massed attack, free flow of information, and the right to question authority are elements that have been credited with the military successes of the West for nearly three millennia. Since the Greeks formed governments early in their history, they were also some of the first to organize an effective army. The states of ancient Greece and Rome were hostile toward one another, so naturally many battles were fought. All male citizens were expected to participate in warfare. But they also had a stake in the outcome; they did not fight only for their king or ruler but for personal freedom and the security of their family, farm, and civilian lifestyle. These ideals allowed them to develop effective armies that fought brutal and short wars using shock tactics, often resulting in severe casualties on both sides. Writers of the Classical World include such personalities as the Greek historian Thucydides, who authored *The History of the Peloponnesian War* between Athens and Sparta in the fifth century BCE, and Roman military and political leader Julius Caesar, who wrote the history of Rome's wars with Gaul in the first century BCE.

From the fall of the Western Roman Empire until the Middle Ages, social and economic reform resulted in new developments in military tactics and weaponry. A feudal system emerged where the king granted land to distinguished soldiers; it was essentially a mix between a military and social organization. The cavalry knightly class developed from this system because only rich noblemen could afford the expense associated with ownership of horses, armor, and weapons.[20] By the time of Carl von Clausewitz, Europe had been through the Protestant Reformation, French Revolution, and Napoleonic Wars.

Based on his experiences of warfare, Clausewitz sought to write a book that identified "the permanent elements of war."[21] He emphasized that various "frictions" such as uncertainty, ignorance, confusion, and fatigue often interfere with one's combat plan and prevents one from exercising full control over the enemy. He believed that a useful theory must include all elements that pertain to battle; not just those that are measurable such as distances, but also the intangibles of morale and common sense. He stated that "[a] critic should never use the results of theory as laws or standards but only—as the soldier does—as aids to judgment."[22] Having participated in combat and suffered the humiliating experience of defeat, he was more concerned with examining the strategic elements of warfare than prescribing scientific measures for its conduct.[23] He viewed combat in relation to its surroundings and recognized that a theory is not a simple thread that links two deductions. Rather than presenting answers through an immediate and utilitarian tool such as a handbook for fighting, he asked questions in the hope of gaining insight into the complexity of conflict. His greatest contribution to military theses may lie in the organization and compilation of commonly known facts rather than in new discoveries.

Clausewitz's interpretation of combat can be attributed in part to his long and varied military career which spanned four decades. Although he was a minor player in the great conflicts of his time, he became a military man at age twelve and saw combat not long thereafter. He dedicated his life to the study of warfare. "In whichever way I might like to relate my life to the rest of the world, my way takes me always across a great battlefield; unless I enter upon it, no permanent happiness can be mine," he wrote in a letter to his fiancée, Countess Marie von Brühl.[24] He served both on the Prussian and Russian front; he endured "heat and dust" and "the lack of food and water," as well as time in captivity.[25] He graduated at the top of his class of forty students from the Berlin War College, or *Kriegsschule*, and was eventually promoted to Major-General. The fact that he did not command troops in battle distanced him from the leadership and allowed him to be critical of the command.

Clausewitz's *On War* has been printed in several editions and languages and has been widely studied at the military academies. This, alone, speaks of its posterity. It was left as a work in progress at the author's death in 1831, to be interpreted and built upon for generations to come. For example, in 1916 and 1917, the British during their attacks on the Western Front relied on using maximum force at the main point to bring the enemy to its knees. By the end of World War I, Clausewitz's principles could be found in the U.S. Army Field Service Regulations. During the Korean War, continued studies of Clausewitz led to grappling with problems of conducting warfare for a limited aim rather than the total overthrow of the enemy. Combat became synonymous with the struggle for peace. The Fleet Marine Force Manual 1, *Warfighting*, first published in 1989, relies extensively on Clausewitzian philosophy. Clausewitz has thus written the most enduring military treatise in existence in the Western world and has shed light on the trinity of conflict: the politics of battle; its physical dimensions (or violence); and the passions of the people (or chance, which makes allowances for the creative spirit).

Although the martial arts as practiced today find many uses including personal protection, sports competition, and self-cultivation, war was historically a political instrument used to compel an enemy to do the will of the victor. How one viewed conflict and developed systems of fighting was part of the political climate. The long military traditions of Asia and Europe contributed to the development of individual combat arts, which evolved from battlefield tactics and strategies used in warfare within and between the countries in the respective regions, and have further been influenced by local cultural beliefs. Their diversity has remained a fascinating subject as evidenced by the great numbers of instructional books, philosophical studies, and accounts of personal experiences that have been written about the traditional Chinese, Japanese, and Korean martial arts, in addition to Western grappling, boxing, fencing, and mixed martial arts. Each martial style displays unique characteristics. The words kung-fu, karate, taekwondo, jujutsu, savate, kickboxing, and pankration, for example, evoke images of Asian and Western customs and lore.[26]

Despite the influences of different cultural beliefs, Asia and the West experienced similar problems with respect to the security of the state and external and internal unrest. Both viewed combat as "a true political instrument" and the highest expression of a person's will to live, "the basis of life and death, the Way to survival or extinction."[27] The differences between Sun Tzu and Clausewitz may at first seem profound. Yet on a conceptual level, their discourse displays far more similarities than differences which further demonstrates that factors such as time period (Sun Tzu and Clausewitz were separated in time by more than two millennia), geographical location (Asia versus Europe), and cultural issues (debated by military historian Victor Davis Hanson in his book, *Carnage and Culture*) are less significant in combat than are an understanding and embrace of a universal human nature. Whether Asian or Western in origin, the different styles of martial arts employ techniques similar in concept and execution. Once individual fighters have corrected for the geographical area (or the modern sports arena) and the "political" situation (or the mores under which one studies the art), they will face similar difficulties with respect to power, deception, confusion, physical conditioning, and morale.

The author acknowledges that the military histories of Asia and Europe are long and complex and that this book merely scratches the surface. However, by engaging in critical study of the respective regions, one can eliminate inappropriate methods of analysis and reach a greater appreciation for the complexity of events that have led us to this day. Rather than emphasizing spiritual paths, "ways of

Chinese bamboo book of Sun Tzu's Art of War, commissioned or transcribed by the Qianlong Emperor (1711-1799 CE). *(Image source: Vlasta2, Wikimedia Commons)*

living," or self-cultivation, this book differs from other philosophical or historical martial arts studies by presenting the military theories behind the development of tactics and strategy in the combat arts. Theory gives structure to fact, relates the past to the present through logical links, and strengthens and refines judgment. Many of the distinct fighting styles that exist have been practiced since antiquity. Others are hybrids or modern inventions. It is not possible to cover all fighting styles or even a majority in a book this size; however, the author hopes that the martial arts surveyed will at least provide a fair sampling of what is available for study to the interested scholar.

Although Sun Tzu's and Clausewitz's powerful assertions will likely challenge common approaches to success and hopefully spark debate, the aim of this book is to establish a solid foundation for further study, decentralize the martial arts, and bridge the gap between the traditional Asian arts and their Western counterparts.

CHAPTER 1

THE NATURE AND CONDUCT
OF COMBAT

"Military tactics are like water; for water in its natural
course runs away from high places and hastens down-
wards. Just as water retains no constant shape, so in
warfare there are no constant conditions."

— **Sun Tzu**

"Action in war, therefore, like that of a clock which is
wound up, should go on running down in regular motion. But wild as is the nature of war it still wears the
chains of human weakness."

— **Carl von Clausewitz**

As mentioned in the introduction, if one wishes to understand the
underlying laws of combat and the effectiveness of the martial arts,
one must examine the historical context under which they developed. The fact that war and violence plagued China for thousands
of years contributed to efforts put forth by the literati and military
men to analyze the principles of war. Sun Tzu wrote the *Art of War*
during the turbulent Warring States period from the fifth to third
century BCE, when the ancient order in China was destabilized
through shifting alliances. Unrest persisted into near modern day
(Shanghai, in the early 1900s, was one of the most violent places

in Asia) and contributed to the growth of the fighting arts. For example, wing chun, a style of kung-fu which focused primarily on defending against political turmoil and guerrilla warfare, was developed during the late Ming Dynasty (1368-1644 CE) for the purpose of fighting the forces of the invading Qing Dynasty (1644-1912 CE).[1] Wing chun practitioners use many short range techniques for trapping an opponent and neutralizing the attack. The art relies on aggressive forward pressure with focus on taking the most direct route from point of origin to target. Note that many Asian martial arts are several thousand years old, while others were introduced more recently. "Judo was born in 1882, and aikido in 1935. Taekwondo and hapkido were introduced in the 1940s and '50s, even though they were based on much older systems."[2]

In the West, Carl von Clausewitz's *On War* was likewise a product of extensive interstate conflict. Although written at a much later date, it had roots in the Western military tradition dating to Classical Greece and Rome with emphasis on pitched battle in open terrain. Certain martial arts, such as ancient Greek boxing, were developed for the purpose of hardening the athletes for war and became brutal parts of Western athletic culture. The boxers were essentially head hunters fighting with spiked gloves. Since they did not fight by weight classification, physical size and strength were clear advantages.

Both Sun Tzu and Clausewitz viewed warfare as a form of political intercourse. When negotiations had fallen by the wayside and war was unavoidable, the state moved forward with the aim of ending the conflict as quickly as possible by attacking the enemy's strategy and crippling his forces. However, political intercourse through physical violence is not limited to states going to war with one another but can be observed in any human group that concerns itself with the distribution of power and authority, and thus extends to individuals engaged in single man combat for reasons ranging from the preservation of honor to the defense of life. As noted by Clausewitz, war is personal combat on a larger scale and a fight should be taken to conclusion often by killing the adversary.[3] Even societies that advocated Confucian ideals fought battles to

Statue of ancient Greek boxer resting on a boulder after a match, from the Thermae of Constantine, third to second century BCE. Note the leather straps used by the boxer to protect the knuckles and increase the damaging power of the strike. *(Image source: Marie-Lan Nguyen, Wikimedia Commons)*

the death.[4] A soldier's commitment to fight could be ensured by rousing his fighting spirit, or *ch'i*, before battle.[5]

This chapter demonstrates that both Asian and Western combat arts were brutal activities designed primarily for fighting an enemy to the death; they were historically not about character building, spirituality, or self-perfection. The conduct of fighting changes with the introduction of new ideas (as observed, for example, when

Royce Gracie won the Ultimate Fighting Championship I in 1993 through the use of Brazilian Jiu-jitsu, and started a trend among martial artists to seek grappling skills), but the nature of fighting remains constant regardless of the scale of the conflict or the types of weapons and techniques used. The nature of fighting is by definition unchanging and comprised of such entities as danger, exertion, uncertainty, and chance.

Key Points: Nature and Conduct of Combat

Sun Tzu	Carl von Clausewitz
War is the greatest affair of state.	War is a continuation of politics by other means.
The best way is to win without fighting; to defeat the enemy through diplomatic means before war breaks out. Force should be used as a last resort.	Victory is achieved through the destruction of the enemy forces; diplomacy is not an element of combat. The use of force is both necessary and effective.
Deception should be used extensively with attacks aimed at the opponent's strategy (his plans).	Attacks are of primary importance and should be directed at the opponent's center of gravity (his critical point or vital area).
War is shapeless like water and requires the ability to adapt.	War is unpredictable and consists of political aims, violence, and chance (friction).

Although Sun Tzu's and Clausewitz's military theories display distinct differences, upon closer examination one can detect several subtle (and not so subtle) similarities in the practice of Asian and Western martial arts. The history and traditions of the martial arts reveal much about the culture of the people, the terrain or environment in which battle was fought, and the type of enemy one expected to face. How war is rendered in ancient Chinese writings is largely a result of Chinese culture. Although Confucian thought and the elevation of the literati over the warrior class contributed to the perception that China was resistant to war, that warfare

could be rationalized and ended without bloodshed, and that conflicts could be solved through diplomacy, or at worst, coercion, any
study of Chinese history will affirm that China was hardly a demili-
tarized country that took no interest in conquest and fought battles
only as defensive measures.

Most of Chinese history is littered with accounts of wars of ex-
pansion as well as wars of unification, battles against invaders, and
the forceful suppression of civil unrest and rebellions. Large por-
tions of the Chinese populace owed military service to the state,
which raised armies with troops numbering in the hundreds of
thousands. Although the wu (military) and wen (civilian) spheres
appear to be separate entities, they were tightly intertwined. The
Ming Minister of War, Tan Lun (1520-1577 CE), said that "to have
wen and not wu is to be a scholar behind the times/to have wu and
not wen is to be an ignorant man."[6] Like the interdependence of
the yin and the yang, military achievement could not exist without
literary virtue, and vice versa. Confucian thinking influenced leaders to seek balance and restore things to their proper places. Although wen was considered a greater virtue than wu, a powerful
man needed both.[7]

The Chinese texts further display a clear admiration for physical strength and boldness in battle. Although the army should be
deployed with restraint, it should be deployed with determination
once the decision was made to fight. It was not unusual in ancient
China to sacrifice whole battalions deliberately in order to outsmart
the enemy.[8] Individuals engaged in single combat with the enemy
were expected to demonstrate valor. For example, openly displaying weapons even if one never used them communicated that one
was well-versed in martial tactics. The Hua Guan Suo Zhuan (the
story of Hua Guan Suo), a recently rediscovered Chinese novel first
printed in 1478 CE, contains a description of the twenty-four battles
that the hero Guan Suo fought. When Guan Yu, Guan Suo's father,
suffered defeat and lost his sword into the deep water of a pond,
Guan Suo who nearly died in battle had an experience of descend-
ing into hell where he was told that he must return for the sword if
he were to score the victory. Following this call of duty, he recov-

ered the renowned sword from the deep water of the pond.[9] War was thus talked about as a restoration of harmony, but killing was its object and boldness its distinguished quality.

The nature of combat or its defining characteristic was evident in the first instant of fighting. A key principle of Sun Tzu's teachings is that war is a matter of life and death, and it is this knowledge that motivates soldiers to fight and win. In single man combat, both fighters know that if neither gives way to the wishes of the other, the battle will be resolved by blood. Achieving victory without bloodshed is the ideal, yet the difficulties associated with such a feat should be clearly understood. As reinforced in the Chinese classic, *T'ai Kung's Six Secret Teachings*, "If you can attain complete victory without fighting, without the great army suffering any losses, you will have penetrated even the realm of ghosts and spirits."[10]

Although Sun Tzu stresses the importance of defeating the enemy through wisdom rather than force, a reason why he had more leeway for diplomacy than Clausewitz is because he wrote about battle before it had erupted, while Clausewitz analyzed it away from its ideal form. It was not compassion that prompted Sun Tzu to advocate winning without fighting, but the turbulent era in which he lived and his sparse resources. When he was appointed commander of the Wu army, he had to fight an enemy, the state of Ch'u in 511 BCE, which was many times larger.[11] He recognized that physical conflict would likely result in heavy losses, which would weaken his forces and prevent him from using full military strength if diplomacy fell by the wayside. War is destructive even for victors and leads to immense suffering, disease, starvation, and death. From the recognition of this fact grew also Sun Tzu's favorable view on deception: to appear weak when you are strong and strong when you are weak. Taking prisoners instead of killing the enemy and convincing them to fight against their own was yet a way to increase the size of his forces, and was not done for the sake of compassion. Had the army that Sun Tzu commanded been numerically superior to the enemy, he might well have chosen a different foundation for the *Art of War*. It is also worth noting that the bureaucratic tradition in China opposed wars on financial grounds, because lengthy military campaigns would divert resources away from civil interests and jeopardize the civilian control of political matters.[12]

The misconception that China was a peaceful country is further grounded in the long battle history with the nomads or steppe people in their relentless attacks on the northern border. In order to place themselves above these "barbarians," the Chinese people thought of their enemies in derogatory terms while promoting a civilized and educated culture at home. The old Chinese adage, "Good men are not used for soldiers, good iron is not used for nails," demonstrates how one thought about the military profession.[13] But this adage did not translate into action, as Chinese swords, for example, were made of the best steel available and were some of the most impressive pieces of weaponry ever crafted. Honorable practices on

Modern sumo wrestlers. In ancient times, the object of sumo was not to win a sports competition but to slay the opponent through brutal tactics including head butting and striking. Like the ancient Greek boxers, sumo wrestlers were selected for their size, which runs contrary to the commonly propagated belief that the Asian martial arts rely on cunning and finesse over physical strength to defeat the adversary. (*Image source: Eckhard Pecher, Wikimedia Commons*)

the battlefield may have been preached by the authorities, but once in the fray, soldiers did what was necessary to meet the demands of the situation. As in any army, they were influenced by feelings of fear, hate, anger, and uncertainty.

Confucian and Buddhist undercurrents are not limited to China but can also be detected in the Japanese fighting arts. For example, shorinji kempo, established in 1947 after Japan's defeat in World War II in an effort to raise the people's spirit, teaches its practitioners to do whatever needs to be done to fend off an attacker, yet suggests that students should never initiate an attack but use the art only in self-defense.[14] However, like their Chinese counterparts, the Japanese martial arts were developed for the purpose of killing the adversary. Sumo, also known as sumai, meaning struggle, its ancient form dating to the first century BCE with the goal of slaying

As demonstrated in this print from the *Bubishi*, an early Chinese document about karate, so-called "dirty" fighting, such as clawing the eyes and pulling the hair, was permissible in the ancient Asian martial arts, which generally did not pit strength against strength but relied on gaining a tactical advantage over a stronger adversary. *(Image source: Wikimedia Commons)*

the adversary, used tactics that included head butting, striking, and stomping the opponent to death.[15] Although some modern martial artists advocate kinder ways of pacifying an attack, for example, by taking the adversary to the ground without hurting him, each fighter would historically use the maximum amount of force available to him.

Jujutsu, or the "gentle art," likewise utilized devastating techniques. (It was the motion, rather than the technique or intent that was gentle.[16]) Unlike judo, which is widely practiced for sports in modern day, the purpose of jujutsu was to give the samurai an option of ending the fight by maiming or killing the adversary with his bare hands. Should he lose his sword in the heat of battle or otherwise be unable to use it, the samurai would strike with his hands or use any means at his disposal. As described by Yamamoto Tsunetomo (1659-1719 CE), a samurai retainer who devoted his life to the service of his lord, "If his [the samurai's] hands [were] cut off, he [would] press the enemy down with his shoulders. If his shoulders [were] cut away, he [would] bite through ten or fifteen enemy necks with his teeth."[17] As demonstrated through this passage, the traditional Japanese martial arts had origins in combat and included plenty of "dirty" fighting. Proper intent when going to war proved important, as reinforced by the famous Japanese swordsman Miyamoto Musashi: "Whenever you cross swords with an enemy you must not think of cutting him either strongly or weakly; just think of cutting and killing him. Be intent solely upon killing the enemy."[18]

Even aikido, which was developed by Morihei Ueshiba (1883-1969 CE) from jujutsu and the sword arts and is sometimes considered not combat or even self-defense but a martial art that encompasses a higher spiritual dimension, is descended from combat arts that were very much intended for use when fighting an adversary to the death.[19] Although the modern martial arts practitioner can find many benefits in the spiritual and sports aspects of his fighting style, according to karate great Fumio Demura, studying only for sport while ignoring the traditional elements of combat would be like studying only two chapters in a book: You will get half the picture but miss the gist of the art.[20] The same holds true for

Chinese martial arts practiced mainly for showmanship or health, such as wushu or tai chi chuan, whose wartime roots should not be forgotten. Wushu literally means military art. And the covert elements of tai chi chuan, intended to prevent the adversary from anticipating when and how an attack will happen, will prevent him from planning a proper defense.[21]

Korean martial arts take a similar tack. As noted by one hapkido master, avoiding combat through diplomacy or by distancing oneself from the situation is the better way. But when the use of physical force is unavoidable, one should strive to end the fight as quickly as possible and strike to vulnerable targets such as the eyes, nose, and throat with the aim of doing damage. Full control is achieved when safety is reached through the destruction of the enemy forces. Ultimately, the measure of success is not whether you neutralize the attack by doing as little damage as possible, but whether you go home to your family.[22]

In the West, tradition and culture likewise influenced how one viewed combat. Citizen soldiers in the Classical World were farmers when not on campaign. Campaigns had to be short since farms needed tending, which meant that battle was often brutal and fought with the goal of avoiding protracted war. Instead of relying on ambush, surprise, or prolonged battle trying to outsmart the enemy, the opposing forces met at a predetermined place and attacked each other head-on. The characteristics of the enemy determined the type of warfare one would fight. In contrast to the Chinese who faced the horse borne Mongols and used long range weapons such as bow and arrow, the Greeks and Romans fought in tight battlefield formations against enemy infantry with swords and other weapons.

Annihilation rather than war of attrition is thus the thread that has run through most of Western combat history. Mixed martial arts have roots in the athletic endeavors of the ancient Greeks. Pankration, which appeared in the Olympic Games in 648 BCE, is an attack-oriented martial style presented as a simulated form of no-holds-barred combat.[23] Although biting and eye-gouging are forbidden, it follows a Hellenic code that includes striking and kicking, submission holds and grappling. The Spartans employed a militaristic style of pankration not suitable for the Olympic Games, because the limitations of the Games, they believed, would have a negative effect on techniques used in live combat.[24] The Romans adopted pankration in the gladiatorial arena.[25]

Pankration, an attack-oriented combat art developed in ancient Greece, displays similarities to the mixed martial arts of today. The fighters use a variety of striking, kicking, grappling, and submission techniques. (*Image source: Matthias Kabel, Wikimedia Commons*)

Brutally engaging the enemy and driving him to exhaustion, yet striving for a positional advantage, can be observed in Western combat sports such as kickboxing. For example, a fighter might kick an opponent's lead leg repeatedly until he becomes apprehensive and tries to protect his leg by switching stance or blocking the kick. The fighter now takes advantage of his opponent's weakness (fear and possibly an unstable stance) by throwing a knockout strike to his jaw. Whether the aim is to kill in actual battle or knock out an opponent in sports competition, the object is ultimately to funnel the forces toward the critical point, which Clausewitz called the center of gravity and which houses the enemy's primary strength. A judo practitioner's strength is his ability to throw an adversary to the ground; a jujutsu practitioner's strength is his ability to execute a joint lock; a kickboxer's strength is his ability to knock out his opponent with a strike or kick. A judoka who takes a powerful strike to the jaw or kick to the legs can no longer exercise his strongest tactics and strategy (a balanced throw); a kickboxer who has been taken to the ground by a judoka or jujutsu practitioner can no longer strike or kick with power.

Clausewitz's emphasis on attacking the critical point should also be referenced to the fighters' relative rather than absolute strength. In other words, he who enjoys numerical superiority can overrun the enemy army. In personal combat, a bigger or stronger person can overrun a physically inferior opponent like a tank, if the smaller person makes the mistake of pitting strength against strength. It is therefore particularly crucial for a person of inferior physical size or build to attack the enemy's center of gravity. Note how this idea corresponds with Sun Tzu's ideal of exploiting the enemy's strength, for example, by yielding to his power and turning it against him, giving the physically inferior fighter a tactical advantage: "[J]ust as flowing water avoids the heights and hastens to the lowlands, so an army should avoid strength and strike weakness."[26]

Although renditions of Chinese battles focus on exploitation of opportunities and subduing the enemy through cleverness rather than physical strength, Sun Tzu was likewise an advocate of funneling the forces against the critical point. On this subject matter, the real test of Sun Tzu's and Clausewitz's theses lies in the definition of the critical point. Sun Tzu believed that the enemy's center of gravity was his strategy or his plans, and foiling his plans would end the battle before it had begun (thus, winning without fighting). Attacking his strategy could also disrupt his focus by sabotaging his momentum. Clausewitz, by contrast, believed that the enemy's center of gravity was his physical strength, and thus the destruction of his forces the primary objective on the grounds that an army that is physically destroyed cannot continue the fight.

Note that although Clausewitz recognized the power of offensive action in breaking the enemy's will to resist by destroying his means to resist, he did not conceive of wars as just or unjust and therefore did not bother to discuss the morality of brutal offense. Since a nation has the right to fight for survival, he viewed all national wars as just. Likewise, when a person's life is endangered or he risks serious bodily harm, fighting, even to the death, is justified. When morals are mixed with combat theories, rules dissolve into vague ideas. The conduct of war and the morality of war must therefore be discussed separately.

Sun Tzu and Clausewitz further recognized the constantly changing conditions of war; Sun Tzu by prescribing unorthodox tactics and the use of deceptive practices, and Clausewitz through the element of chance which can strike either belligerent and requires an ability to adapt. Sun Tzu took an abstract tack by comparing war to water: "And as water has no constant form there are in war no constant conditions."[27] Like water, which takes the path of least resistance, the fighter should adapt to the terrain and circumstances and plan his strategy accordingly. Those skilled at using unorthodox strategy can provide a ceaseless number of surprises and become as "inexhaustible as the great rivers."[28] Two millennia later, the Japanese swordsman Miyamoto Musashi compared combat to the elements of nature: ground, water, fire, wind, and void, and noted that, "[w]ater adopts the shape of a receptacle. It is sometime a trickle and sometimes a wild sea."[29] It is from the water principle that formlessness is derived, or the idea that an army that has no set form cannot be defeated.

Since the nature of water dictates a downhill flow from high to low, from full to empty, a skillful military strategist preserves energy by going with the flow of the attack, countering to that which is "empty," such as an opening in the opponent's defense or a weakness in his stance, with conquest of the adversary coming by way of yielding to his power. Unlike Western boxing or wrestling which pits strength against strength and where physical size is a virtue, yielding to the opponent's power allows a smaller or weaker person to defeat a bigger adversary, and is one of the core principles that makes the martial arts effective for men and women of inferior strength. Examples of the water principle can be observed in aikido, where the practitioner avoids frontal assault and blends with the opponent's motion, redirecting his momentum, and taking advantage of his energy. Aikido also teaches mental flow. The purpose of *mushin*, or no mind (also the absence of thought), is to facilitate natural flow of body movements in order to speed up reflexes and reaction times.[30] Once the martial artist has redirected the opponent's attack, his mind is ready to manage the next threat by avoiding prolonged fixation on the initial attacker. Judo, the art of throwing an opponent, likewise relies on blending the physical body with the flow of motion, joining one's center of gravity with the opponent's and thus combining both fighters in single motion.

Although aikido and judo fall under the category of "soft" arts, many martial arts in Asia were developed to break bones and end the fight as quickly as possible. They were not about humiliating the adversary or teaching him a lesson while letting him walk away physically unscathed. Flow, or taking the path of least resistance, is found in the brutal joint lock techniques of hapkido. The greater an adversary's struggle against the lock, the greater is his pain. Every joint lock has a counter, yet a skilled martial artist can flow with the opponent's motion and guide the "offending" limb into an excruciatingly painful position. A person well-versed in joint locks can almost always find an opportunity for transforming one lock into another as the need arises, using the opponent's motion to tighten the lock and ultimately ending the encounter with a break or dislocation of the joint.

The water principle as used in hapkido also relates to relentless determination. Like the persistence of dripping water, which will eventually bore a hole in stone, the hapkido practitioner penetrates the opponent's defenses while avoiding the direct power of his attacks. As described by hapkido grandmaster Bong Soo Han (1933-2007 CE), "There is an old saying: 'To catch a tiger, you must go to the tiger's lair.' So in defense, to be effective, you must flow with the opponent. You must read his force—this will let you know what force you must apply as the appropriate counter."[31] Yielding to the force further relates to the Confucian and Daoist concept of yin and yang. Strong techniques are received gently, and gentle techniques are countered with powerful strikes. Crude techniques and strong contact result in clashing energies and create "double-weightedness, a condition that . . . violates the yin and yang . . . because both weapons [or fighters] are exerting yang force simultaneously."[32]

What is sometimes overlooked by the Western martial artist is that references to water, earth, birds, tigers, and other animals and elements of nature which are often found in the names of Asian martial arts techniques demonstrate an influence of local culture, tradition, religion, and philosophical thought. Confucianism, Daoism, and Buddhism propagated the belief that man is part of nature, and that nature is comprised of interacting forces that must be in balance to restore harmony. Just as life leads to death, war is the path to destruction but also the path to peace. Talking about techniques in terms of nature; for example, how to block an attack by "parting the wild horse's mane,"[33] may seem confusing to the Western martial artist. But the technique differs only on the philosophical and not practical level. The Western martial arts utilize many techniques that are almost identical in execution to their Asian counterparts yet go by different names. For example, a reverse punch and a front kick can be found in most martial arts regardless of their place of origin.

In the same vein, although Sun Tzu used the word *shuaijan* (snake) for describing a successfully deployed army—"If you strike its head the tail will respond, if you strike its tail the head will respond. If you strike the middle both the head and tail will react"[34]—he used the word as an analogy and did not mean to say that the army must study the movements of a snake in order to reach success in war. The *Questions and Replies Between T'ang T'ai-Tsung and Li Wei-Kung* further reveals that the meaning of heaven, earth, wind, clouds, dragons, tigers, birds, and snakes were not cleverly created formations in the images of animals, but code names for secret techniques:

> The ancients secretly concealed [their] methods, so they craftily created these eight names . . . Dragons, tigers, birds, and snakes originated in the distinctions of the platoons and squads. Later generations erroneously transmitted them. If they were cleverly creating formations in the images of animals, why would they stop at eight?[35]

Clausewitz viewed war as violent action and its defining characteristic unpredictability as a result of chance (friction) and human weakness. However, as those who are well-versed in the martial arts know through experience and empirical evidence, any theory or battle plan will likely fall apart when the first blows are exchanged. Although action in war will run down in regular motion and each move is designed to bring the martial artist closer to the objective, the means employed are intended to help him reach a defined end. Taking advantage of the enemy's plans, position, and weapons, and adapting to changing circumstances is crucial to success. Again, Clausewitz underscored the importance of attacking the enemy's center of gravity: "If the enemy is thrown off balance, he must not be given time to recover. Blow after blow must be struck in the same direction . . . by constantly seeking out his center of power, by daring all to win all, will one really defeat the enemy."[36]

Now that we have gained basic insight into Sun Tzu's and Clausewitz's battle philosophies, before proceeding with a deeper analysis of the martial arts it is important to acknowledge that war is an element of being human and is neither Asian nor Western in nature. A simple way to test this concept is by noting how a martial artist with some training under his belt can fight using Sun Tzu's and Clausewitz's principles of combat, even if he has never studied either strategist. Neither Sun Tzu nor Clausewitz introduced anything new in their writings but merely brought to light what has always existed. Despite the fact that they were separated in time by roughly 2,500 years and lived in different geographical regions, we can observe several similarities. For example, both Sun Tzu and Clausewitz discussed the importance of strategy, of laying the plans and mounting an attack when the enemy is weak. "It is the rule of war," Sun Tzu stated, "if our forces are ten times the enemy's to surround him; if five to one, to attack him."[37] In a similar vein, Clausewitz stressed that "[t]he first rule [of war], therefore, should be: put the largest possible army into the field."[38] Both Sun Tzu and Clausewitz gave weight to the natural flow of combat, its unpredictability and human weakness; Sun Tzu by relating war to water, yielding to the opponent's power yet penetrating his defenses; and Clausewitz by recognizing the different tempos in fighting, the spurts and lulls in action, and the adjustments that must be made in accordance with the enemy's capability to resist.

Although common stereotypes and popular notions of Asian and Western martial arts are often propagated, they are based on a superficial understanding of the history of war and strategic thought. Martial arts as different as taekwondo and wrestling were developed to answer the problems of their respective regions and circumstances, yet have roots in the common laws of combat. Human nature remains constant; thus, Clausewitz's observation that war contains certain "permanent elements," which, "on the basis of a realistic interpretation of the present and the past," can be formed into a "comprehensive theory."[39] Or as described several centuries earlier by Italian political philosopher Niccolo Machiavelli (1469-1527 CE): "Wise men say, and not without reason, that whoever wishes to foresee the future must consult the past; for human events ever resemble those of preceding times. This arises from the fact that they are produced by men who have ever been, and ever shall be, animated by the same passions, and thus they necessarily have the same results."[40]

At the core, combat is about forcing an enemy to succumb to one's will. We might use different sets of weapons (in the martial arts, for example, empty hands, stick, or knife), and these weapons may eventually become outdated. But the experience of warfare, or the characteristics by which one recognizes combat, remains unaltered. The nature of war and the conduct of war are interdependent. The practical techniques used for defeating an enemy in combat (the conduct of war) cannot be developed unless one also understands the physical and mental elements of being human and which shape the nature of war. It is this recognition that has given Sun Tzu's and Clausewitz's writings such longevity. Their theories are based on a philosophical understanding of war and represent a nuanced approach to conflict that can be adapted to many forms of fighting. Hand-to-hand combat instructor W. Hock Hochheim grasped this idea well when he said:

> The martial arts come in flavored packages. Strip them to the core and you'll find many of the same techniques and strategies. Watch a fight that involves an Indonesian silat expert, a Japanese jujutsu master and a French savate fighter, and even though they will be dressed differently and might enter into close quarters differently, when it comes time to throw down, their physical steps will be similar. Those similarities are the universal tactics that constitute the essence of combat.[41]

As has been demonstrated in this chapter, Asian and Western martial arts originated as a result of threats to one's life, but have been altered to suit participating civilians in modern society and often include elements of confidence building, spirituality, and sportsmanship. Martial arts in China date as far back as the time of the Yellow Emperor, from the twenty-sixth to the twenty-seventh century BCE. For example, the martial art of shuai chiao (also called "the mother of kung-fu") includes striking, grabbing, and throwing techniques and was deemed brutally efficient. Although its roots extend to the military training exercises conducted during the reign of the Yellow Emperor, by the third century BCE, the art had become popularized and was practiced as entertainment also among civilians. A subset of the same art involves grabbing and throwing the attacker to the ground in the quickest way possible.[42] Likewise, the original goal of the Korean martial art of taekwondo, which origins can be traced to the Koguryo Dynasty founded in 37 BCE, was not sports or exercise, but to destroy the enemy and end the threat, preferably quickly through a single kick or technique.[43]

In the West, wrestling, which is several thousand years old and may be considered the most archaic form of fighting, no longer permits the practitioners to use techniques that were once designed to permanently injure or kill the adversary, such as joint twists against the knees or ankles, or techniques designed to break the opponent's back or neck. Even no-holds-barred contests have been adjusted to minimize the risk of permanent injury or death by prohibiting biting, eye-gouging, and other severe techniques. These changes, which have made the fighting arts accessible to civilians, do not diminish the fact that the martial arts were developed for combat, often to the death. According to Tamas Weber, a decorated veteran of the French Foreign Legion, who has studied the martial arts since 1951, "The bottom line is that karate-do is a violent art. Because of the times of peace we are living in, however, a part of that art can be used as an enjoyable sport activity. The important point here, though, is not to lose the direction and real meaning of the training."[44] As echoed long ago by Thucydides, an ancient Greek historian of the fifth century BCE, "Peace is best secured by those who use their strength justly, but whose attitude shows that they have no intention of submitting to wrong."[45]

CHAPTER 2

WHAT IS COMBAT?

"A state that has perished cannot be restored, nor can the dead be brought back to life." — **Sun Tzu**

"War is no pastime; no mere passion for venturing and winning; no work of a free enthusiasm."
— **Carl von Clausewitz**

War is a serious activity not to be taken lightly, and neither Sun Tzu nor Carl von Clausewitz suggested that one should rush into action before exhausting the alternatives. But when combat is inevitable, a comprehensive and scientific analysis of the situation should be conducted to create a set of workable guidelines for battle. As Sun Tzu said, "The victorious army first realizes the conditions for victory and then seeks to engage in battle."[1] Now that we have gained an overview of the nature and conduct of combat, we will define combat and proceed to examine the various elements of military action: tactics and strategy, offense and defense, and ultimately how to secure victory.

Although both Sun Tzu and Clausewitz attempted to bring structure to the nature and conduct of war, a common and recurring question is what constitutes combat or martial arts. Is it, as Clausewitz suggested, about forcing one's will on the adversary? Is it about winning the battle even if the war is ultimately lost? Or is it about diplomacy or humbling the adversary by giving him certain desirable insights into the seriousness of conflict without engaging him in physical battle? Can an Asian and Western martial artist understand each other's strategy and tactics? Or does understanding require specific expression, reflecting the cultural mindset of the warrior as learned through history and tradition?

Definitions are important because they produce expectations of what the participants should accomplish, and by what means. While some people argue that martial arts, in order to be classified as such, must be Asian in character and contain certain philosophical elements, others hold the view that Western style boxing and wrestling are also martial arts. However, since the word "martial" is of Latin origin, it is unreasonable to suggest that people of Asian origin would use a word with the exact same connotations when describing their fighting arts. Whether we call it martial art, fighting art, combat science, or self-defense also has to do with the art's primary usage. Some martial arts, like bujutsu, the fighting art of the samurai class in Japan, were developed for use by armies of professional warriors on the field of battle. Others, like karate in Okinawa and some styles of kung-fu in China, were developed for use by the general populace.[2]

Other difficulties with definition arise from the argument over how much of the art is "art" and how much is science. Although samurai retainer Yamamoto Tsunetomo emphasized that "the person who practices an art is an artist, not a samurai, and one should have the intention of being called a samurai,"[3] did he really mean to say that combat is scientific rather than artistic or creative? A problem with ancient literary works is that nuances tend to get lost in the translations.[4] A specific word, such as force, can have different connotations and mean, for example, strategic military power or brute force. To further illustrate the difficulty associated with defining war and combat, one might note that the United States *Department of Defense Dictionary of Military Terms* lacks a definition of both.

It can nevertheless be established that a student of karate, taekwondo, jujutsu, hapkido, and other traditional martial arts must study the history and culture, as well as a range of techniques and forms, if he is to reap the full benefit of his studies. By contrast, martial arts that were developed primarily for the military battlefield of today or for street defense, such as krav maga and other reality based self-defense eclectic styles, tend to be more limited in scope (although not necessarily less effective) by teaching techniques that are simple to learn and easy to remember when performed under stress, and that work against a variety of attacks. Those who benefit the most from the study of these types of fighting arts are generally specialized groups of people, such as law enforcement, military, or rape prevention specialists rather than the general populace. As stated by Jim Wagner, a police and military defense-tactics instructor, "People who must fight for a living quickly learn to depend on a streamlined arsenal of proven techniques."[5]

Sun Tzu reminded us in the first paragraph of the *Art of War*, that war "is a matter of life or death," and should therefore "be studied thoroughly."[6] Clausewitz likewise recognized that nations are built through violence and continue to relate to each other through violence, and that war is a normal state of human existence. This chapter defines combat by examining its destructive elements, the value attached to the initiative, and its scientific and creative components. It distinguishes between ideal and real war, and demonstrates the importance of knowing your enemy and yourself in order to counter the effects of friction and chance.

Key Points: What is Combat?

Sun Tzu	Carl von Clausewitz
War is destructive; it is a means to an end and is fought for a political objective.	War is an act of violence and sometimes blind instinct, and is fought for a political objective.
War involves seizing the initiative and attacking the enemy from a position of strength.	Success in war requires offensive action and seizing the initiative.
Combat requires knowledge of your enemy and yourself.	Numerous "frictions" determine the outcome of battle. Knowing the enemy is easier said than done.

War is based on intellect and ability to outthink the adversary, and is comprised of interaction between physical and mental forces.	War is primarily art and not science, and requires intellect and understanding of the human spirit.

War is destructive even for victors. Engaging an adversary in battle should therefore be done only after careful consideration, when there is a serious threat to one's safety, and as a means to an end and not an end in itself. Although Sun Tzu and Clausewitz wrote from the perspective of mass armies, their respective theories apply to individuals engaged in single man combat and are easily

Judo practitioner imposing his will by attacking his adversary's center of gravity; in this case, his opponent's balance. (*Image source: Lance Cpl. Scott M. Biscuiti, Wikimedia Commons*)

transferrable to practitioners of the martial arts. Sun Tzu said, "Generally, management of a large force is the same as management of a few men . . . And to direct a large force is the same as to direct a few men."[7] As reinforced by the Japanese swordsman Miyamoto Musashi, the "spirit of overcoming others" is the same regardless of whether you are fighting a thousand opponents or just one.[8] Clausewitz likewise compared war to a *Zweikampf*, or duel, between two people and recognized that "war is nothing but personal combat on a larger scale," with the purpose of forcing the opponent to succumb to one's will.[9]

Whether you are a karateka, judoka, sumo wrestler, or boxer, the goal is ultimately to defeat the adversary by imposing your will on him through a strike or kick, takedown or throw, by pushing him out of the ring, or by attacking with such overwhelming force that you destroy his fighting spirit and compel him to surrender. Ideally, all moves should be done on your terms. In competition, points should not simply be scored, but should be scored well. The skilled martial artist seizes the initiative, presses the attack, and takes advantage of weaknesses in an opponent's defense by attacking his center of gravity.

Shotokan karate, founded in Okinawa by Gichin Funakoshi (1868-1957 CE), is a no-nonsense hard style that relies on straight strikes and kicks with the bodyweight behind the blows. As such, it demonstrates the value of seizing the initiative through linear moves and determined offense. Circling the opponent is done mainly as a diversion. The purpose is to "kill" the adversary or end the fight with a single blow, with each technique fully developed for maximum effect. Although a chief priest at the Buddhist Enkaku-ji Temple in Kamakura, Japan has written on the memorial to Gichin Funakoshi that "there is no first attack in karate," one should remember that seizing the initiative refers to a fight that has already begun when the option of walking away no longer exists. When the opponent commits to the attack, the defender seizes the initiative, for example, by timing a strong front kick to the adversary's advance, catching him in the midsection and knocking him to the ground as he moves forward. Gichin Funakoshi said:

When there are no avenues of escape or one is caught even before any attempt to escape can be made, then for the first time the use of self-defense techniques should be considered. Even at times like these, do not show any intention of attacking, but first let the attacker become careless. At that time attack him concentrating one's whole strength in one blow to a vital point and in the moment of surprise, escape and seek shelter and help.[10]

While both Sun Tzu and Clausewitz stressed the importance of seizing and holding the initiative and striking the enemy at a time when he does not expect it, Sun Tzu believed that a conflict could be brought to conclusion successfully through a combination of factors, including politics, economics, and diplomacy. Protracted war should be avoided, because it was a drain on the resources and fighting spirit of the people. Striking the enemy preemptively was therefore acceptable, as long as one had conducted a critical examination of the situation and determined that an attack against the enemy's plans, alliances, or forces would shorten the duration of war.[11]

Clausewitz likewise believed in avoiding protracted conflict but discounted diplomacy as an element of war.[12] Combat, by definition, must include a physical engagement or else it is not combat. Battles should be fought to the finish. In Clausewitz's mind, the idea that martial arts are purely acts of self-defense would have been an absurdity. The "character of battle, like its name, is slaughter (the German word, *Schlacht*, means both [battle and slaughter]), and its price is blood." Although it has the capacity to break "the enemy's spirit more than it [takes] lives," the object is to dominate the adversary by acting with concentrated force, quickly and without pause, and outfight rather than outwit the opponent.[13] As reinforced by the United States Marine Corps *Warfighting* Manual, initiative and physical domination of the enemy must be present in order for it to be war:

At least one party to a conflict must take the initiative for without the desire to impose upon the other, there

would be no conflict. The second party to a conflict must
respond for without the desire to resist, there again would
be no conflict . . . We can imagine a conflict in which
both belligerents try to take the initiative simultaneously—as in a meeting engagement, for example. After the
initial clash, one of them will gain the upper hand, and
the other will be compelled to respond—at least until able
to wrestle the initiative away from the other. Actions in
war more or less reflect the constant imperative to seize
and maintain the initiative.[14]

However, violence is not necessarily chaotic madness. Imposing
one's will on the adversary brings purpose to conflict and justifies
the use of force. Consider a self-defense scenario, attempted rape,
or kidnapping. While the adversary is trying to impose his will on
the victim, he or she is simultaneously trying to impose his or her
will on the adversary as an element of defense. The person who
succeeds at dominating the other wins the battle. Although the
martial arts are frequently marketed as self-defense, once conflict
is under way and one cannot escape, initiative and offensive action
are needed to win. If neither fighter in a martial arts competition
is willing to take the initiative and engage the opponent, there can
be no competition. In fact, martial artists have on occasion been
disqualified in tournaments for failing to engage, running from the
opponent, prolonging the fight by purposely spitting out the mouth-
piece, or showing timidity. When a martial artist enters a competition, it is assumed that he has come to fight by physically imposing
his will on the other fighter. To further demonstrate a point, after
the opponent, taken down by a leg hook, attempted to escape the
boundaries of the fighting arena at a judo tournament in California
in 2006, Brazilian Jiu-jitsu fighter Royce Gracie dragged him by the
belt and one leg back to the center of the mat. Although refusing to
engage the adversary in competition is considered a negative martial arts trait, outside of the competition arena restraint should be
used. As Clausewitz and Sun Tzu reminded us, war is no pastime
and the dead cannot be brought back to life.

A preplanned approach to victory lends strength to the idea of seizing and holding the initiative, but depends on the ability to adapt to changing circumstances when plans are foiled. Sun Tzu and Clausewitz agreed that knowledge of the opponent's objectives (such as winning by point or knockout in sports competition, or robbing, raping, maiming, or killing on the street) is crucial in order to achieve victory. Without this knowledge, one cannot determine the conduct of battle or the tactics and strategy, because one cannot define what victory means. Furthermore, victory cannot be secured unless the martial artist understands his physical and mental capabilities, the opponent's objectives, and, perhaps most importantly, what is worth fighting for. Assessing the environment and political climate to determine if it is supportive of your cause allows you to establish insights into your and your opponent's respective strengths and weaknesses. Royce Gracie deceived his opponents in the Ultimate Fighting Championship, because nobody believed that this person of a rather small physical build would have the capacity to beat a bigger opponent. But the same deceptive practices do not work every time. Once Gracie had revealed his strengths, his opponents learned how to exploit them in future tournaments.

In order to bring further meaning to the definition of war, fighting should be viewed as neither a complete science (knowledge) nor a complete art (ability to utilize knowledge). Science is the act of knowing, and art is the act of doing. Science requires theoretical education. But art, as a rational process and a mark of intellect and character, requires practical experience and judgment.[15] Since war is a conflict of interest, it adheres to a balanced relationship between science and art. Sun Tzu recognized this relationship through the *cheng* (the physical or conventional forces) and *ch'i* (the mental or creative forces). Compare, for example, physical strength or power as derived from size and momentum with power as derived from proper timing. A martial artist who has the benefit of size may choose cheng, or conventional forces, to overrun the opponent; if not, he may choose ch'i, or unconventional forces, to lure the opponent forward into a perfectly timed counterstrike. Sun Tzu said, "When torrential water tosses boulders, it is because of its momentum; when the strike of a hawk breaks the body of its prey, it is because of timing." Both have their place in the martial arts. A skilled fighter can display the physical potential of a "fully drawn crossbow," and simultaneously exercise timing that is as sharp as "the release of the trigger."[16]

Note that although Sun Tzu relied on a prescriptive rather than descriptive theory of warfare, it is unlikely that his intent was to memorize an answer to every problem. A more plausible explanation for this approach is that he wanted to provide the reader with the ability to recognize "identifiable, recurring patterns as they emerge."[17] Many of his ideas are not deeply developed in writing, yet have intellectual depth which forces the reader to interpret and think about the scenarios inherent in each idea. Rules should thus be guidelines to which the martial artist applies his or her judgment.

Clausewitz likewise understood the relationship between science and art, and the creative element inherent in warfare by recognizing that the "step is always long from cognition to volition, from knowledge to ability."[18] Although he used scientific terms such as friction and center of gravity in his descriptions of war, they were meant to be used as analogies and not relied upon in a literal scientific sense. He professed that no set prescription for success exists. During his service at the War College in Berlin in 1818 and 1819, he criticized the program for being too focused on rote learning, which he believed would hinder individual initiative and adaptation.[19] Physical combat, he stated, is the only way through which one can make sense of war, because "the state of circumstances from which an event proceed[s] can never be placed before the eye of the critic exactly as it [lies] before the eye of the person acting."[20]

The soldier thus takes the weapons he is handed and does the best he can with what he has available at the time of the engagement. He is not interested in the technology behind weapon making, for example, at least not as a primary reason for his profession. Likewise, the martial artist has two hands and two feet which he uses for striking, kicking, grabbing, and trapping while adapting through creative means the best he can. While his only concern may be blocking a strike as the enemy reaches out toward him, he may realize that he can trap the arm instead and execute a lock against the wrist, bringing the enemy to his knees and ending the fight. A martial artist who gets knocked to the ground unexpectedly while raising a leg to kick, may find an opportunity for trapping the opponent's lower legs and bringing him down. It is this creativity which occurs at the spur of the moment that relates to the art of war. As reinforced by the nineteenth century German military historian Max Jähns (1837-1900 CE):

> [T]he science of war describes the means available to wage war at any given time and derives from them theories on how war should be conducted. It can never reach an ultimate form because the means are constantly changing. It is, therefore, [a] (science of experience) rather than a science of external truths. The art of war, by contrast, is the application of a theory of war to specific situations and requires creativity and intuition on the part of the practitioner which cannot be taught.[21]

The relationship between science and art suggests that the reality of war cannot be measured through theoretic learning alone. The martial artist can read any number of books and watch any number of instructional videos, but if he fails to gain practical experience he will never fully understand the combat arts. Timing, for example, can be understood in a theoretical sense, but it takes considerable practice to acquire it. Or as martial arts instructor Keith Vargo says, "Science can help us understand and improve our arts," but it takes art to sum up "the fighting skill of an individual."[22]

Even as a balance is struck between science and art in training, the enemy's will is difficult to control and the element of chance can strike either belligerent. In ideal war, all moves are interrelated and advance one closer to victory. Ideally, the attack should be directed at the heart of the enemy's strength, using maximum concentration of force and avoiding pauses. In the martial arts, ideal war can be related to a kick or punch combination. Consider first if the combination is logical. For example, would a roundhouse kick naturally follow a strong side thrust or spinning back kick and still be effective when kicking a live target? Would the opponent be in position to absorb both kicks, or would he be too close or too far away? Would an uppercut logically follow a front kick, or would the distance to the target be inappropriate?

Ed Parker's (1931-1990 CE) style of kenpo karate uses checks and strikes to secondary targets designed to position the opponent's body for the finishing blow. One might check the adversary's arm, for example, in order to bring his body forward to receive a reverse ridge hand strike to the throat. Although the idea is sound, it only works if the opponent reacts as intended to the set-up strike. All unforeseen factors will quickly render theory insufficient, as you will learn when your training partners deviate even slightly from the prescribed attack. If the attack calls for a right punch and your partner throws a left punch instead, or a right punch to a different target than the one called for, or a kick, the specific defense you have practiced will not work as prescribed. You must now adapt instantly, using your creative forces to secure victory.

Although Clausewitz like Sun Tzu took an abstract tack in his analysis of war, he recognized that combat reflects the uncertainty of the real world and did not attempt to describe a metaphysical world. Nor did he profess that it is possible to reach an ideological solution to conflict. Studying strategic principles allows the martial artist to evaluate what is ideal and what is real in combat, and discover that how we talk about war is not how it ultimately happens. The martial artist must be prepared to make modifications when passing from theory to reality. While the intent is to "cripple the enemy's forces, so that he cannot, or cannot without danger to his existence, carry on the [battle]," combat is susceptible to chance and the nature of conflict is inherently unpredictable.[23]

Although the physically inferior fighter seldom wins over a much stronger enemy—as stated by Sun Tzu, "When ten to the enemy's one, surround him. When five times his strength, attack him. If double his strength, divide him"[24]—a revealing example of the unpredictability of battle as seen in the Ultimate Fighting Championship I, might be sumo wrestler Teila Tuli losing a tooth and getting cut by the eye a mere twenty-three seconds into the fight despite the fact that he carried a significant weight advantage over his opponent. Moreover, war cannot be bloodless precisely because it cannot be reduced to an exact science. The fact that the Ultimate Fighting Championship quickly became a blood bath because nobody knew what to expect from anyone else further demonstrates the unscientific nature of combat, and also spurred the development of rules in future tournaments, including mandatory gloves and a ban on kicking or kneeing the head of a downed opponent.

Does the fact that combat is unpredictable mean that everything you have learned according to prescribed patterns of training in the martial arts is useless? The answer is an unequivocal no. Since the purpose of theory is to cast light on events, recognize relationships, eliminate ignorance, and separate the important from the unimportant, studying the many possibilities in advance coupled with extensive practice allows the martial artist to narrow the risk that something will go significantly wrong. In short, a good theoretical base alongside sensible practical training allows one to execute sound judgment when danger strikes and determine the scope of the battle before taking action. The victory is thus prepared in the planning, and herein lies the importance of Clausewitz's suggestion that one should not take the first step without considering what might be the last. Clausewitz and Sun Tzu were in agreement that one should engage the enemy only after one has studied his strengths and weaknesses and determined that the chances of victory are reasonably good. Thus, the victorious fighter realizes the conditions for victory before engaging in battle.

In contrast to ideal war, in real war the moves cannot be fully predicted. Actions must therefore be modified upon passing from theory to reality. Real war is waged for the purpose of achieving minor advantages for their own sake without necessarily considering them direct steps toward victory. While ideal war focuses on the constant and determined movement toward the destruction of the enemy's forces (or fighting ability), real war consists of a number of separate battles and includes pauses or standstills in action. Victory can also be achieved through peace negotiations rather than direct attack. The defining characteristic of real war is what Clausewitz called "friction." Friction can take the form of physical frictions such as difficulties with the environment or weapons, or mental frictions such as fatigue or loss of morale. All action in war is based on probability. Although you may know yourself, your strengths and weaknesses, at best you can only make an educated guess about the cards your opponent is holding.

Sun Tzu acknowledged the effects of friction and the many possible forms that battle can take when he said that "[t]here are no more than five musical notes, yet the variations in the five notes cannot all be heard."[25] As noted previously, he recognized that armies of overwhelming numerical superiority or strength should not be fought. However, heeding this advice may not be possible in a street fight, mugging, rape, or robbery because it assumes that you are the instigator of battle and alone decide whether or not to proceed. A weakness of Sun Tzu's *Art of War* is that it fails to consider the fact that you do not have monopoly on initiative, deception, flexibility, or concentration of force at the decisive point, and that the enemy may resort to the same tactics. Friction, or the uncertainty of conflict, applies to all parties. To Sun Tzu's credit, however, he appears to have recognized this weakness when he said, "It follows that those skilled in war can make themselves invincible but cannot cause an enemy to be certainly vulnerable. Therefore, it can be said that, one may know how to win, but cannot necessarily do so."[26]

Although how to proceed in combat at any given moment often proves to be a gamble and friction can sabotage the best-laid plans, a consolation might be that chance does not strike one belligerent exclusively but can also create opportunities that can be exploited for personal gain. For example, you might face a very aggressive opponent in a kickboxing match and come through the first round feeling lucky if you merely prevent him from knocking you out in subsequent rounds. Halfway through the second round, your opponent unexpectedly loses steam perhaps as a result of having failed to attain proper cardiovascular conditioning. It is this friction, this unexpected occurrence that allows you to land a strong blow to his jaw, knock him out, and win the match.

In their definitions of war, both Sun Tzu and Clausewitz included the surrounding conditions and circumstances: the geography and technology, the social and political climate, and one's passions and ambitions. An important point to consider is that Sun Tzu did not write about battles between states, but about conflict within his own culture where the enemy would likely resort to predictable tactics. His ideas would be quite applicable, for example, to the Ultimate Fighting Championship the way it was originally intended, for the purpose of exposing weaknesses within particular fighting arts. An aikidoist was expected to use only techniques applicable to aikido; a taekwondoist would rely only on techniques he would normally practice in the dojang; a kickboxer was expected to use only techniques he would resort to in a sanctioned match between two kickboxers, thereby making combat predictable and suggesting that it is possible to officially declare "superiority" of one art over another. As discussed previously, the event quickly "deteriorated" into mixed martial arts, where a fighter could use any techniques or blend thereof he chose regardless of his background or training.

The objective of the Ultimate Fighting Championship, fought inside the octagon, was initially to pit one style of martial art against another to determine which style was superior. This is an unjust way of evaluating the martial arts, because it fails to consider the historical context under which they were developed. *(Image source: Lee Brimelov, Wikimedia Commons)*

Furthermore, part of the difficulty associated with reconciling Sun Tzu and Clausewitz and their respective views on warfare lies in the particular era and culture in which they lived. Deception, for example, although strongly emphasized by Sun Tzu and promoted as a useful tactic in traditional martial arts and street defense alike, was difficult to use during Clausewitz's time in the midst of the in-dustrial revolution when warfare was waged by mass armies. More-over, our tendency to view the martial arts within the framework of certain common trends and generalizations commonly bring misun-derstandings both to traditional approaches to combat and the "newer" mixed martial arts. A traditionalist, for example, might hold the view that a mixed martial artist is a brawler who lacks in-sight and depth, while a mixed martial arts practitioner might sneer at the traditionalist, claiming that he would be ineffective in a "real" fight. One might thus ask: Does a martial art express the culture of its country of origin? Or does it merely express the needs to meet the political situation that existed at the time of its development? Which arts are applicable to modern combat, which are timeless, and which are merely anachronistic recreations of a particular cul-ture and historical time frame?

History will attest that most countries of the world have inte-grated military systems. For example, even though infantry might dominate warfare, cavalry has historically proven more effective for scouting and breaking up enemy formations, or for meeting certain forces that did not rely on foot soldiering such as the Mongolian invasions of China in the thirteenth century CE. The martial arts are likewise integrated systems of fighting. A successful fight con-ducted outside of established conventions seldom relies exclusively on stand-up or ground combat, empty hands or weapons. By blend-ing several principles typically found in karate, judo, and aikido, the Korean martial art of hapkido has managed to fuse physical and mental power, the cheng and the ch'i. It offers a good example of a traditional martial art operating as an integrated system of fighting by drawing power from karate, leverage from judo, and flow or the principle of diverting the opponent's motion from aikido.[27]

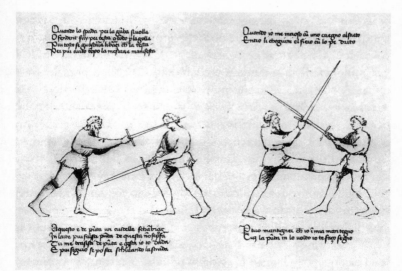

Quanto lo spada per la giuba fuolla
O fordent filij per testa o tudo plagolla
Du tofto se questua libiai ch la testa
Per pui auto tepo la mefura e manifesta.

Quanto io me meuofo cu uno cueguo alfucto
Ento li choguini el fiero cu lo pe duito

Aquesto e de pum un curtelle sebatriar
In laite pus fulpa pum de quefta nofuffa
Tu me trafliffa depuita e gafta io io dutru
E puffeguto se poffa fibiluanto lafimila

P tuo manhagna ch io i mia man tegno
Cuz la pum in lo uolto io te fugo fegno

Medieval European swordsmanship was an integrated system of fighting that used kicks and grabbing maneuvers to achieve the objective. Note the front kick displayed in this medieval sword fighting manual. *(Image source: Francesco Novati, Wikimedia Commons)*

Similarly, the ninjutsu practitioner of feudal Japan had to master a wide variety of weapons such as daggers, shuriken (throwing stars), and brass knuckles, along with implements such as ladders and hooks that allowed him to scale walls. In addition to basic empty hand skills such as striking, kicking, and grappling, he was trained in stick and staff fighting, swimming, and horsemanship or combat from horseback. This made ninjutsu a truly integrated martial art.[28] The Japanese samurai and the medieval European knights likewise employed integrated systems of fighting; the samurai by resorting to jujutsu skills if he could no longer rely on his sword, and the European knight by resorting to kicks to keep an opponent at sword's range, or grabbing, trapping, and dagger skills when at close range.

Thus, knowing that the ideal type of battle will rarely be fought, how does one offset the effects of friction? Although friction cannot be eliminated, it can be managed through proper preparation, or as Sun Tzu said, "Know the enemy, know yourself; your victory will never be endangered. Know the ground, know the weather; your victory will then be complete."[29] Actual combat experience will undoubtedly assist in strengthening instinct and preparing for uncertainty. Consistent and tough training might be the next best alternative. Doctrine, or a syllabus designed to meet the specific needs of the situation, further allows one to establish guidelines for conduct that assist judgment. Although fighting cannot be learned through theoretical study alone, theory sheds light on the many phases of combat and acts as a guide to train judgment through critical inquiry. But to remain effective, theory has to "remain realistic: it cannot allow itself to get lost in futile speculation, hairsplitting, and flights of fancy."[30] Learning to step at an angle of 26.5 degrees when executing a defensive technique against an opponent's strike is an example of a hairsplitting flight of fancy. Learning the concept behind the technique—to step at an angle away from the path of power—would prove more practical.

Although Sun Tzu and Clausewitz came from vastly different backgrounds, their teachings complement rather than contradict each other. Sun Tzu focused on what to do in each unique situation; Clausewitz analyzed why things happened and left the reader to decide how to act. While Sun Tzu would have offered the sound advice to withdraw from a conflict with superior speed in order to avoid pursuit, Clausewitz would have questioned whether the circumstances for such a withdrawal were possible. Both approaches are needed in order to wage war successfully, because it is not possible to settle for a specific action unless one also has a clear idea of what one is capable of doing at any particular moment. Furthermore, Sun Tzu was primarily concerned with the conduct of war on the higher philosophical level; Clausewitz with the conduct of war on the operational level. Despite their different approaches to conflict, both Sun Tzu and Clausewitz recognized that combat is unpredictable and brutal and should not be taken lightly. Both agreed that the reality differs from the ideal way of waging war.

CHAPTER 3

PREPARING FOR BATTLE

"It is a doctrine of war not to assume the enemy will not
come but rather to rely on one's readiness to meet him."
— **Sun Tzu**

"Habit gives strength to the body in great exertion, to
the mind in great danger, to the judgment against first
impressions." — **Carl von Clausewitz**

Sun Tzu underscored the importance of knowing your enemy and
yourself in order to create a tactical advantage in battle. A defined
combat plan raises morale by decreasing the element of surprise. It
thus behooves the martial artist to define the challenge and study
the opponent's strategy and fighting habits prior to an upcoming
competition. Granted, a surprise attack on the street, or a true
tournament where you will be fighting several opponents until the
last man is standing, makes it difficult to apply this concept. Yet
proper preparation through disciplined drill will raise your courage and turn the odds in your favor. As acknowledged by Tsutomu
Ohshima, founder of the Shotokan Karate of America Organization, no amount of encouraging words, only consistent training, can
give the fighter the mental fortitude he needs to meet an enemy in
a struggle of life and death.[1]

Ch'i, described by Sun Tzu as the will and intention to enter
battle, is attained by defining the objective, assessing the situation,
and physically preparing for the engagement. Organizing military

Terra Cotta soldier and horse. The thousands of life-size clay figures guarding the tomb of the First Emperor of Qin demonstrate the importance one placed on military preparedness in China. *(Image source: Wikimedia Commons)*

campaigns through this sequence of events translates into clarity of vision. Coupled with skill and accuracy, it leads to confidence and fighting spirit.[2] The Terra Cotta army, comprised of thousands of life-size clay figures guarding the tomb of the First Emperor of Qin who died in 210 BCE, demonstrates the importance one placed on military preparedness in ancient China. As reinforced nearly two thousand years later by Emperor Qianlong (1711-1799 CE) of the Qing Dynasty, whose long lasting reign resulted in great expansions of China's boundaries, "Indeed, soldiers may not be mobilized for one hundred years, but they may not be left unprepared for one day."[3]

In Europe, drill likewise built courage and confidence and helped soldiers come to terms with the uncertainties of war. Carl von Clausewitz acknowledged that combat plans tend to fall apart once the first blows are exchanged, yet fortune favors those who come prepared. The various frictions he described can be overcome at least partially through routine work and genuinely tough training. Although he emphasized physical strength directed at the opponent's center of gravity, or the balance point against which an attack will cause the enemy to collapse, moral strength, or the ability to operate efficiently in the face of adversity, is gained through habitual training. Habits are built through drill. Drill is built on prescribed patterns of training that bring the martial artist to a position of familiarity under stress. Recognition and knowledge of these patterns lead to mental strength and fortitude. We have thus come full circle, or back to what Sun Tzu identified as ch'i.

In ancient and modern times, specific exercises have been used to prepare soldiers for the demands of the battlefield. It was well understood that he who had superior physical strength and endurance had a better chance of surviving the rigors of war than he who did not. In personal combat, a muscular and supple body that communicates strength and readiness to fight can also give one psychological control over the enemy. The exercises used in ancient times to build a fighter who was strong in body and spirit differed not too much from those relied upon today. Training and drill are keys to combat efficiency; their purpose is to develop a fighter who can endure and win. This chapter demonstrates why habitual exercises increase physical skill, mental discipline, and courage, and help the martial artist perform with precision in the training hall and in encounters of life and death.

Key Points: Preparing for Battle

Sun Tzu	Carl von Clausewitz
Proper preparation leads to skill and accuracy, which further lead to fighting spirit.	Military spirit is created through direct experience in war or through severe training.
Battles are won or lost in the preparation.	Fortune favors those who come prepared.
Discipline and synchronization of forces result in superior power.	Decisive and synchronized application of force leads to superior power.
Repetitive drill develops courage and ability to act without conscious thought or self-awareness.	Habitual training eliminates the need for critical thought and is central to building courage and confidence.

Intense training prepares the martial artist to endure physical and mental hardship. Endurance, in turn, leads to combat efficiency. Although also serving a ceremonial function, the purpose of drill has historically been to prepare troops for battle and familiarize them with the conditions under which they must fight. General Wu Ch'i of Wei of the Warring States period said, "Now men constantly perish from their inabilities and are defeated by the unfamiliar."[4] In addition to giving armies the capacity to maneuver large forces efficiently into positions that maximize power, drill is meant to closely mimic the tactical moves individual soldiers are expected to use on the battlefield and allow them to respond to commands without hesitation. As movements are perfected and mistakes minimized, drill instills confidence. As confidence grows, pride, poise, and a sense of team spirit follow. Some historians consider near modern China's contempt for drill for fighting purposes central to China's loss to Japan in the Sino-Japanese war of 1894-1895 CE:

[T]he lack of drilling not only undermined the effectiveness [of] the firepower of the Chinese troops despite very good weapons, but it also undermined the discipline of the army and its commitment to fight. In this respect, the Chinese army stood in stark contrast to the Japanese army. [T]he importance of drill lies not only in enhancing the effectiveness of firepower and the efficiency of the army, but also in improving the discipline and morale of the army.[5]

In contrast to the above statement, discipline in ancient China was valued to the point that capital punishment was inflicted on those who refused to act as prescribed. As recorded in the *Spring and Autumn Annals of Wu and Yüeh*, Sun Tzu was brought before the King of Wu to demonstrate how to form untrained troops into attentive and cohesive combat units. He first ordered the king's three hundred concubines to form into an army, with two of them acting as company commanders. After ensuring that they had received instruction in military methods, he had the company commanders order the rest to assemble, advance with their weapons, and deploy into military formation. When the women covered their mouths and laughed, Sun Tzu informed the king that if the instructions were not clear and the soldiers did not act as directed it was the fault of the commanding officers. Failing to lead and instill discipline in the troops was punished by decapitation. He then had the two concubines acting as company commanders decapitated. The next time Sun Tzu beat the drums and ordered the women into military formation, they advanced and withdrew "in accord with the prescribed standards without daring to blink an eye."[6]

Sun Tzu further related in the *Art of War* that the reason why soldiers were taught to perform in unison and remain focused on the task at hand was to prevent fear and desertion caused by excessive thought: "Now, gongs and drums, banners and flags are used to unify the action of the troops. When the troops can be thus united, the brave cannot advance alone, nor can the cowardly withdraw."[7] Consider your *dojo* or training hall. When drilling the basics and shouting loud *kiais* (or kihaps) in unison with your peers, the group absorbs your identity and contributes to each person's individual power. Historically, the kiai might have stemmed from a reaction to danger and an effort to summon assistance from friends. In a similar manner, when gongs or drums are sounded before a kung-fu competition, it gathers the audience's attention and unifies the people, raising the spirit of the fighters. It may also place fear in the opponent. Most people will agree that the sound of gongs or drums has a psychological effect on fighters and audience alike by bringing purpose to action. Music or drums have served important functions in all military cultures by instilling discipline and fighting spirit in the warriors. The ancient Chinese classic, *The Methods of the Ssu-Ma*, explains how a soldier, "when he enters the army and takes control of the drumsticks and urgently beats the drum he forgets himself."[8]

While the victory is prepared in the planning by studying the political situation, the terrain, and the fighting habits of the respective armies, drill and constant repetition of techniques give the soldiers the skill to make quick and resolute decisions when crisis strikes. In accord with knowing yourself and your enemy, Sun Tzu asked us to think about in which army, yours or the enemy's, regulations and instructions are better carried out, and "[w]hich army has the better trained officers and men."[9] Forces must be synchronized to defeat the enemy quickly and with minimum wasted motion. Consider how a perfectly timed strike in the martial arts with all your body's mass behind it may seem almost effortless, yet has the power to knock out your opponent. "[T]he energy of troops skillfully commanded in battle," Sun Tzu observed, "may be compared to the momentum of round boulders which roll down from a mountain thousands of feet in height."[10] As reinforced by Chinese military strategist and statesman Zhuge Liang (181-234 CE) in his classic text, *The Way of the General*:

> In military operations, order leads to victory. If rewards and penalties are unclear, if rules and regulations are unreliable, and if signals are not followed, even if you have

an army of a million strong it is of no practical benefit. An orderly army is one that is mannerly and dignified, one that cannot be withstood when it advances and cannot be pursued when it withdraws. Its movements are regulated and directed; this gives it security and presents no danger. The troops can be massed but not scattered, can be deployed but not worn out.[11]

Drill and ritualized training, such as striking or kicking the air, mitts, or bags repeatedly also benefits the martial artist because it accustoms him to the rigors of combat, trains his body and mind to endure hardship, and teaches men and women of different backgrounds and temperaments to use their martial art judiciously. The common rules of dojo etiquette in the traditional martial arts include displays of courtesy such as bowing when entering or leaving the training hall and prior to and following technique practice and

Karate training at Shuri Castle, Okinawa, 1938. Synchronization of movement, which is achieved through drill, is valuable to the individual martial artist because of the power it provides. The perfect stance, for example, gives you balance, enabling you to transfer force from your foundation to the strike or kick through hip rotation. *(Image source: Nakasone Genwa, Wikimedia Commons)*

free sparring; wearing a traditional uniform or *gi* to impart integrity and reverence for the art; and lining up according to rank. Many martial arts schools also employ some kind of oath or creed intended to promote reflection on the art, such as an affirmation of one's intention to develop discipline and only use the art for the defense of self and others.

When speaking of drill, we do not only mean punching, kicking, and blocking, but also static exercises such as stance practice and meditation. A military recruit or sentry who has to stand at attention for long periods of time, in heat and cold, in rain and snow will at first find the exercises unbearable. But each session brings him more confidence and the belief that he can endure until the end, as his body is strengthened and his mind learns to control his emotions. The martial arts student who is made to stand in a continuous horse stance will likewise steel his body against pain and discomfort, and his heart against distractions and boredom. Such motionless practice instills perseverance and heightens one's senses to the surroundings. For example, in feudal Japan, the ninjutsu fighter, known for espionage and clandestine practices, needed patience and ability to move about in the environment without risking detection. Walking noiselessly through grass or vegetation required superb balance and total control of muscle movements as he carefully shifted the weight from one foot to the other. Once you get used to drill, whether stance practice or technique training, you may even begin to find it relaxing, because it teaches you to respond to commands without hesitation, effortlessly and without excessive thought, and enables you to do the techniques required of your art in the most efficient way possible.

Drill further helps prevent injury and instill confidence by minimizing fear. Ch'i, a fundamental concept of the Asian fighting arts, relates to the physical and metaphysical realms. "The ancient Chinese created the character for ki [ch'i] using the radical for 'gas' or 'steam' and the radical for 'rice.' Noticing the steam rising up from the boiling rice inspired the notion of something material out of this world and something really not there."[12] Passages in Chinese writings further describe ch'i as vitality, the breath of life; and also the mist, smoke, or cloud formations rising from the enemy's positions, which shape and direction of flow will predict the outcome of battle. However, ch'i can best be understood, perhaps, if thought of as fighting spirit. Your goal is to use your high spirit to destroy your opponent's morale. As explained by Hirokazu Kanazawa, a renowned karate teacher, there is a strong connection between breath and fighting spirit. For example, most of us are familiar with the idea of exhaling at the exertion of a move. If you participate in contact sparring, you also know that taking a strike to the abdomen or solar plexus while inhaling may drop you to the ground. The *kiai* yell teaches you to tighten your abdomen at the exertion of a technique or at the reception of a blow, and decreases the risk of injury. Thus, "[i]f your breathing is wrong, your body will be wrong and your mind will be wrong."[13]

Furthermore, a clear understanding that you can lose your life in a physical confrontation should prompt you to take your training seriously and eliminate wasteful practices. Shouting and tensing at the moment of impact even when striking the air, communicates to a potential opponent that your techniques are powerful enough to kill, or at least end the fight. One Hapkido master suggests training as if your life depended on it. For example, if your opponent chokes you, be determined in your escape, because you only have seconds to execute it and walk away with your life intact.[14]

Although some say that ch'i fails to mesh with reality and "won't save you from a beating,"[15] the ancient text of the Chinese military classic, *Wei Liao-Tzu*, notes that victories were not divinely inspired, but "were a matter of human effort." If you fail, there are practical reasons, for example, because you are undertrained or "the walls are high, the moats deep." Ch'i is not something mysterious, and "[p]utting spirits and ghosts first is not as good as first investigating [your] own knowledge."[16] Sun Tzu reinforced this statement when he noted that "fore-knowledge cannot be elicited from spirits, nor from gods, nor by analogy with past events, nor by astrologic calculations. It must be obtained from men who know the enemy situation."[17]

The martial artist attains ch'i by conducting an honest assess-ment of his strengths and weaknesses, and through regular training that accustoms the body and mind to the strains of combat. Kata (forms practice) in the traditional Asian martial arts is a valuable training device that spurs the development of fighting spirit. Since people were largely illiterate, kata were essentially "books" that en-abled techniques to be passed down to future generations. Further-more, many techniques in ancient times were meant to work against an opponent wearing armor and had to be modified when practiced against unarmed training partners. Kata allowed a student to prac-tice techniques that could kill without harming his partner.[18]

In addition to conditioning the body for the moves required of the martial art and giving the fighter endurance through extended practice, kata developed mental discipline by teaching precision in technique and instilling muscle memory and ability to act un-der stress. Perhaps most importantly, kata helped the martial arts practitioner form habits which allowed him to take a definite stand in battle and avoid confusion and uncertainty. He could now act without conscious thought or self-awareness, confronting his fear of death and drawing strength from the Buddhist concept of nonat-tachment. In China, emptiness, as when the mind is not obscured or confused, as explained in *T'ai Kung's Six Secret Teachings*, allowed one to discern things that were not manifest,[19] and proved effec-tive, for example, in deceptive practices requiring the anticipation of battle. The moment the soldier established individual identity, the principle of nonattachment would fall by the wayside. In Japan, as taught by samurai retainer Yamamoto Tsunetomo in the "lesson of a downpour," when accepting one's fate, one can remain tranquil even in death: "A man, caught in a sudden rain en route, dashes along the road not to get wet or drenched. Once one takes it for granted that in rain he naturally gets wet, he can be in a tranquil frame of mind even when soaked to the skin."[20]

Technique practice according to prescribed patterns and prear-ranged sparring complement kata by familiarizing the martial artist with combat, making fighting instinctive, and eliminating excessive thought. At the lower levels, techniques are done in unison according to a standardized pattern to train certain body mechanics in the beginner martial artist, allowing him to draw strength from his peers. As we advance, techniques can be changed to suit our individual talents and inclinations. "For an art to be alive," as explained by martial artist and traditional Chinese medicine physician Mark Cheng, "it must be functional for a variety of people, each with his own attributes and weaknesses."[21]

Since ancient martial arts practiced today are still evolving, we naturally see a wide range of variations within an art. However, the basic principles and combat applications are retained. For example, China, the birthplace of kung-fu, has seen this ancient art develop and branch into several hundred distinct styles; although, not all emphasize combat. Originally referring to any great skill (if a person were skilled at calligraphy or cooking, for example, one would say that his kung-fu was good), kung-fu and its many internal and external variations was designed to develop mental strength and physical fighting prowess, reflecting the culture of the particular region in which it was practiced. People from the arid steppes of northern China naturally practiced a different variation of the art than people from the more forested southern regions; thus, the distinction between northern style kung-fu (linear attacks based on strength and speed) and southern style kung-fu (circular attacks based on intricate footwork and timing).[22]

Kung-fu practitioners may train in tactics as varied as long range strikes and kicks with a swift closure of distance and power derived from the waist and shoulders, to acrobatic styles employing mainly high kicks, or close range fighting involving relentless attacks to the legs. The Shaolin method of Chinese boxing, which emerged from the Shaolin Temple near Zhengzhou City Henan Province, was particularly known for its rigorous training practices which focused on strength, speed, and flexibility. The word kung-fu, which refers to an unerring devotion, fostered the idea that in order to be in control of a combat art, one must dedicate oneself fully to its purpose and train with intent. First then can it be said that one's kung-fu is good. Although a skilled kung-fu practitioner would travel to different regions and learn from a variety of teachers, he would naturally favor a few specific hand, foot, or weapon techniques, which he would master to perfection.[23]

Because of its remote location, the Shaolin Temple was prone to attack by bandits, and its inhabitants felt prompted to learn kung-fu for self-defense. Using everyday tools and farming implements as weapons, the monks established a long and rigorous training regimen in self-defense tactics. Learning a strong stance gave them the power to withstand an opponent's attack. To maintain strength, it was argued, stance, although basic, must be practiced for an hour or two everyday throughout the martial artist's life. There are no shortcuts in kung-fu. Only total devotion and endless practice lead to powerful techniques. Other exercises, such as slapping water in a barrel hundreds of times on a freezing cold day, were developed for increasing mental toughness, which was often considered more important than physical toughness. Kung-fu is based on a methodology of constant repetition to instill muscle memory and make

Gate of the Shaolin Temple, known for its disciplined and rigorous martial arts training and drills. (*Image source: Cory M. Grenier, Wikimedia Commons*)

each action second nature, giving the martial artist the power to act and respond automatically and in the most efficient way possible when under threat.[24]

In modern China, sanda, a form of freestyle boxing based on traditional kung-fu, is taught to the roughly two million soldiers of the Chinese military, the largest standing army in the world. Relying on the four tactical elements of punching, kicking, grabbing, and taking the adversary to the ground, for example, by catching his kicking leg and sweeping his supporting foot, sanda is a modern incarnation of ancient mixed-style kung-fu and wrestling and displays many similarities to Western kickboxing and Muay Thai. Although the traditional Asian martial arts are often portrayed as gentler and more compassionate than their Western counterparts, Asian records talk about approaching any combat situation with a readiness to kill. The sanda training regimen, focusing on stamina, physical strength, proficiency in technique, and the acquisition of a mental edge over the adversary is grueling and undertaken in accord with the Chinese saying, "train either in the hottest days in summer or the coldest days in winter."[25]

The West has historically employed many concepts nearly identical to the Asian practices. Military spirit acted as a guide to the individual soldiers when clear directions were missing. According to Clausewitz, there were two ways in which to create spirit for this purpose: frequent wars or severe training.[26] Conceptually, repetitive drills performed in the Western armies, including today's armed forces, differ little from kata and the prearranged training patterns of the traditional Asian martial arts. Military drill, like kata, teaches attention to detail while making movements responsive to outside stimuli. As Clausewitz pointed out, "War is the realm of physical exertion and suffering. These will destroy us unless we can make ourselves indifferent to them, and for this birth or training must provide us with a certain strength of body and soul."[27] When thoughts of death crept into the soldier's mind, he was no longer an effective fighter. Repetitious training according to prescribed patterns has historically allowed soldiers to fight in large formations, by coordinating movement and eliminating cowardice and desertion.

It was also reasoned that men who were too independent generally did not have the caliber to be good soldiers in mass armies; they could not fight well as a team and were unwilling to take orders or endure the punishment that came with disobedience. When men in formation came to realize that they were not a unit but individuals with hopes, dreams, fears, and desires, thoughts of desertion would manifest. The armies of Classical Rome were particularly known for valuing and standardizing drill through disciplined ritual and training, which would hold the phalanx together, allowing it to amass maximum power at the critical point.

As explored in chapter 2, Clausewitz further noted that knowledge of combat is easy to articulate but difficult to apply, and that which is unfamiliar can easily lead to perplexity and inability to act with determination. A fighter who has practiced a particular technique only once has a clear advantage over he who has no familiarity with the technique at all. But repetitive drill that largely eliminates the need for critical thought is ideal over piecemeal practice, and is instrumental in building confidence and freeing the martial artist from doubt. As stated by the Greek general and historian Xenophon in the fourth century BCE, "[W]hichever army goes into battle stronger in soul, their enemies generally cannot withstand them."[28] As reinforced two and a half millennia later by former West

Stranglehold. Practicing your martial arts techniques with intent will give you a near realistic experience and spur proper reactions. *(Image source: Cpl. Benjamin M. George, Wikimedia Commons)*

Point psychology professor Lt. Col. Dave Grossman, "The student's experience in training helps to take some of the surprise out of it when the real situation arises. Effective training also elevates the student's sense of confidence."[29] Martial art training done with intent using at least some physical contact will spur familiarization with potential combat situations. For example, if an adversary grabs you in a rear choke, you will know not to panic and hopefully react with the defensive technique you have learned without further thought.

The need to respond to uncertainty and changing conditions requires talent, or innate ability, which the martial artist can nurture by engaging in relevant training maneuvers prior to battle. Physical preparation may even be more important for preparing the mind than preparing the body for combat, teaching one to act rationally and with determination when under attack. As stated by military historian John Keegan, "That aim, which Western armies have achieved with remarkably consistent success . . . is to reduce the conduct of war to a set of rules and a system of procedures— and thereby make orderly and rational what is essentially chaotic and instinctive."[30] Uncertainty will rob a fighter of his spirit, as will fatigue. You may be an exceptionally talented martial artist with twenty years experience under your belt, but when fatigue overcomes you, all of the techniques you have learned and practiced to perfection will instantly become useless. The risk of premature fatigue decreases with intense physical training, thus giving you the mental edge you need to defeat the adversary.

Practice must also be extensive enough to make the moves habit when performed under stress where fine motor skills tend to deteriorate. Instructors of the Israeli hand-to-hand integrated combat system haganah (defense) take advantage of habitual training patterns by limiting practice to a few techniques, bringing the fighter to a point of familiarity under stress no matter what type of attack he is defending against. The art's effectiveness is derived from the fact that each technique focuses on achieving a common objective, such as taking an empty-handed opponent to the ground without going down with him or unarming a weapon-wielding opponent with the intent of restraining, incapacitating, or killing him.

For example, if you are engaged in a knife-on-knife altercation and the opponent attacks with a slash toward the left side of your neck, you might block his knife hand, slash his wrist, slash his abdomen, stab to his kidney, and slash his leg to take him down and prevent him from continuing the fight. Now, let's say that his initial attack misses because you anticipate it and moved your upper body to the rear. The opponent may now try to counter with a backhand slash to the right side of your neck. But since you have learned to create a point of reference, you know that you are in position to use the same defensive sequence as you would have used had you not moved away from the initial attack: Block his knife hand, slash his wrist, slash his abdomen, stab to his kidney, and slash his leg to take him down and prevent him from continuing the fight. The only difference is that the first defensive sequence is done from an angle along the opponent's centerline (inside technique), while

U.S. Marines practicing the knee strike. If you learn the martial arts by creating a point of reference, as done in the Israeli haganah combat system, your muscle memory will tell you after sufficient practice that a simple technique such as the knee strike can be used any time you are in position to grab the opponent's neck. *(Image source: Sgt. James R. Richardson, Wikimedia Commons)*

the second defensive sequence is done from an angle away from his centerline (outside technique).

The same principles can be applied to an empty hand technique. If the opponent attacks with a right punch, you might block the strike to the inside of his arm and then grab his neck and knee him in the groin. If he throws a left punch, you might block the strike to the outside of his arm and then grab his neck and knee him in the groin. You know that your defense will work because you have created a point of reference (a familiar situation) that tells you that every time you are close enough to block the opponent's strike, you are also in position to grab his neck and throw a knee to his groin or abdomen, no matter what his original intent.

The drills you practice in the training hall are thus designed to improve fighting skill, reflexes, aggression, purpose, and conditioning (physical and mental). However, they are not meant to prepare you *exactly* for how the battle will go down. Clausewitz stressed that there is no single standard that guarantees success in warfare, and even "mercenaries and forcibly controlled peasants" can prove just as effective, for example, as the citizen-soldiers of Revolutionary France.[31] You can test this principle by rhetorically asking who will win a street confrontation: a black belt martial artist or a street thug who has never set foot in a dojo. Ultimately, how successful you are depends on a variety of factors, such as the intensity and intent of your training, your physical size and health, and various frictions, such as fatigue and surprise.

Furthermore, a prearranged defense to a particular offense; for example, a block followed by a front kick as defense against the opponent's punch, should be done with the understanding that the drill is merely one of many possibilities. Free-play exercises that approximate the conditions of combat and promote independent thinking are also necessary to reach success in the art of war. Repetitive drill and training along with critical analysis prior to battle decrease the risk of making irrational decisions that lead to dangerous losses. To increase analytical skill and learn to adapt to changing circumstances, set aside time in the training hall for asking, "What if?" and analyze the possible motivations behind an attack prior to the engagement. Does the adversary want to rob you? Rape you? Humiliate you? Kill you? Does he act out of self-preservation? Does he merely respond to a threat or a perceived threat? If you remove the threat, might there be no fight and you can both walk home safely?

The lesson one should learn is that, although it is not possible to ensure victory through training alone, proper preparation familiarizes the martial artist with events that will likely occur on the field of battle or in the sports arena and decreases the risk of going forward blindly. As Clausewitz stressed, one should start from the reference point of the ideal, yet acknowledge that the battle plan will need to be modified. The more familiar one is with the situation, the greater the chance of reaching success. French emperor and military leader Napoleon Bonaparte (1769-1821 CE) may have had a valid point when he said that "the moral [courage and fighting spirit] is to the physical as three to one." A clear definition of the goal along with good preparation will bring you closer to the ideal form of war by giving you confidence and ability to get back on track when things go awry. Additionally, a person who is rightly prepared has truly considered the complexity of the situation at hand and understands the challenges. You will have a better experience in the dojo if you succumb to the ritualized training practices, than if you question the validity of every move the instructor asks of you. According to Clausewitz, the trick when the losses one suffers on the battlefield undermine courage and fighting spirit is "to make the experience of battle work to the benefit of morale."[32]

As demonstrated in this chapter, both Asian forms practice and Western drill are important for preparing the martial artist for the disorder of the battlefield and the sports arena. Habitual training gives you the power to act instantaneously without thought in the midst of chaos. Whether we call it kata, *poomse*, shadow boxing, or bag work is less important than is its purpose to instill discipline, determination, and courageous performance without thoughts of injury or death. Although actual trials in combat will increase your confidence and enable you to come to terms with uncertainty, British military historian Basil H. Liddell Hart (1895-1970 CE) reminds us that there are "two forms of practical experience, direct and in-direct—and that, of the two, indirect practical experience may be the more valuable because it is infinitely wider."[33] Since a soldier or martial artist has few opportunities to gain direct experience in combat, disciplined and semi-realistic training exercises with one's peers are "infinitely wider" and, therefore, the best alternative.

CHAPTER 4

ELEMENTS OF TACTICS AND STRATEGY

"All warfare is based on deception."   — **Sun Tzu**

"Surprise is the most powerful medium in the art of war."
                              — **Carl von Clausewitz**

As demonstrated in the previous chapters, the martial arts can be divided into preparations for combat and acts of combat. A fight is seldom concluded through one decisive move, however, and both fighters will consider the other's actions and adapt accordingly. Strategy is the master plan that creates the conditions for battle, but the fight is ultimately won through a set of tactical moves that progressively lead the martial artist closer to the goal. Tactics are used to advance the political objective and must be employed with purpose. Since the risk of injury or death in war has historically been great, one must avoid wasteful practices and know the enemy well enough to understand whether or not victory can be achieved. Or as Sun Tzu reminded us, "Act when it is beneficial, desist if it is not."[1] Carl von Clausewitz likewise stressed that the probability of victory must be on your side before you decide to engage in battle. This is true whether or not you are holding an advantage in physical strength.

Before taking action, one must further determine the opponent's objectives, study his strategy, and decide what motives are worth fighting for. A martial artist engaged in competition, might discover that the opponent, a taekwondo practitioner, prefers kicks to hand techniques and generally throws his kicks high. If taekwondo is the primary art of both fighters, the best high kicker may win. But if one fighter favors kickboxing, he might decide to undermine the opponent's foundation by kicking his supporting leg the moment he raises his foot off the ground. If the taekwondo practitioner is carrying his hands low, it might invite the kickboxer to exploit this weakness by positioning away from the attack line and striking the head. Although the kickboxer's strategy involves negating the opponent's strengths and taking advantage of his weaknesses through superior positioning, the particular body part (hand or foot) used to target the head and the particular way by which it is done relate to tactics.

If engaged in a more serious life or death drama where a weapon is involved, your strategy might be to neutralize the threat (the opponent's weapon hand) before attacking a vital target (his eyes, throat, or groin), and then ensure that he cannot continue fighting by taking his foundation. Your strategy is your grand plan. Note that nothing has been specified with respect to how you neutralize the threat, attack a vital target, or take the foundation. These are elements of tactics and refer to the particular moves you use within the fight, such as strikes, kicks, and sweeps. Thus, your strategy (neutralize the treat, attack a vital target, take the foundation) leaves a number of options to choose from. For example, you might trap the opponent's weapon hand, strike his eyes with your fingers, and dislocate his knee with a kick in that order. But you would not attack his forearm after you have disarmed him, because his forearm is not a vital target and would not advance you closer to the objective of rendering the opponent harmless. Knowledge of the enemy is crucial in order to determine what kinds of tactics to use and whether or not the battle is worth fighting. Different tactics will be employed depending on the enemy's political objective. Does he want to rape or kill you? Does he want your wallet?

A fighter who develops good strategy but cannot execute it tactically is not likely to succeed in single man combat. If the tactics are poor, you cannot hope that the strategy will save you. And if the tactics are poor, you are unlikely to be successful in the art of war. You will not always know what types of tactics to use prior to engaging an opponent in battle, however. But he who is well-trained in the use of different tactics and understands the strategy can adapt during the fight and still reach the objective. This chapter demonstrates that when the strategy has been determined, tactical planning must be adapted to fit the changing circumstances of battle. Or as Sun Tzu said, one should "take the field situation into consideration and act in accordance with what is advantageous."[2] Clausewitz agreed. Due to the uncertain nature of war, one cannot predict the enemy's actions from one moment to another but must remain flexible enough to adapt.

Key Points: Elements of Tactics and Strategy

Sun Tzu	Carl von Clausewitz
Deception is most valuable when practiced on the strategic level before the outbreak of physical battle.	A state can rarely surprise another during the preparations for war. Deception has a greater chance to succeed on the tactical level.
The victory is prepared in the planning through an understanding of the enemy's plans and expectations.	Wars are won through a series of tactical moves that lead you progressively closer to the objective.
Know the enemy and yourself. Proper planning is achieved through reliable intelligence and is the key to victory.	Knowing the enemy is ideal, but combat is dominated by friction and the initial plan is almost always unreliable.
Attack the enemy's strategy (his plans). A surrounded enemy should be presented with a way to escape.	Press the attack and destroy the enemy's center of gravity.

Those who excel in warfare rely on a strategic configuration of power. According to Sun Tzu, skilled strategists are "like a fully drawn crossbow; their constraints like the release of the trigger."[3] Strategy is about determining when, where, and how the tactics will be delivered. The reason why strategy (or advance planning) is important, perhaps particularly in a martial art that relies overwhelmingly on the physical engagement, is because good strategy allows the martial artist to break the opponent's resistance physically and mentally before deploying the specific techniques that end the fight. The victory is thus prepared in the planning.

A good strategist can engage a numerically superior enemy with inferior strength and still be successful. As noted in chapter 1, Sun Tzu emphasized diplomacy over physical battle and regarded the ability to break the enemy's resistance without fighting the apex of excellence. But diplomacy, the art of playing to the opponent's interests, works only if one first acquires a thorough understanding of his needs and desires. Even then, there are times when diplomacy will fall by the wayside because the price is greater than the value. This might be the case, for example, when your life is directly threatened. Sun Tzu advised us to fight courageously when on "desperate ground."[4] Moreover, the person who attacks you has likely determined beforehand that he has the capacity to beat you. When he brandishes a knife, it is in the belief that you will succumb to his will.

What should you do? You may start by attempting to calm the situation through diplomatic means, by assuming a non-threatening stance, keeping your distance, asking that he puts the knife away, offering him your wallet, or apologizing for whatever offense he is accusing you of. But if none of this works and he advances toward you nevertheless, decisive physical action is necessary. If you too have a knife or weapon that you can show the opponent, you may be able to shift the leverage in your favor. The opponent, knowing that he will not walk away unscathed, may now find the time ripe for diplomacy and take you up on your attempt to resolve the conflict without bloodshed.

Although Clausewitz was not against diplomacy per se, he considered combat the only effective means by which to win a war. One of his key recommendations involved attacking the adversary's center of gravity, the balance point of his collective strength. For example, a taekwondo practitioner who is exceptionally well-versed in high and powerful kicks will be at a physical loss the moment you take him down through a brutal attack to his supporting leg. When you destroy his physical capability to kick, you will simultaneously sabotage his courage and fighting spirit and thus break his resistance mentally. In fact, a martial artist's center of gravity may well be his mental strength. Clausewitz stressed that the moral elements of battle (courage and fighting spirit) are "completely fused" to the physical forces: " . . . we might say the physical are almost no more than the wooden handle, whilst the moral are the noble metal, the real bright-polished weapon."[5] Victory requires more than good technique. Humiliating the adversary or breaking his confidence may be the strategy you choose for subduing an aggressive opponent.

The purpose of strategy is to break the opponent's resistance. Attacking his center of gravity; in this case his ability to kick high, by timing a front kick to his midsection each time he raises his leg to kick will rob him of his fighting spirit. (*Image source: Alain Delmas, Wikimedia Commons*)

Whether or not you achieve the objective is the ultimate judge of whether your strategy is sound or flawed. When the objective is clear, the strategy can be executed through the use of proper tactics. However, the possibility exists that the tactics, the tools you use to reach the objective, prove unsuitable for the particular opponent you are facing. Using a hook punch to neutralize the hook punch of a good boxer, for example, will merely pit strength against strength. Using upper body movement, a bob and weave, to neutralize his hook punch and establish a superior position away from his attack line followed by a strike to his jaw to knock him out, demonstrates a sounder use of tactics. It may also be that the taekwondo practitioner you were fighting earlier, whose trademark is the high and powerful kick, has superior speed, coordination, and timing due to extensive practice and knocks you out before you get within range to take him down through an attack to his supporting leg. Although the victory is prepared in the planning, the various frictions of which Clausewitz spoke tend to interfere with the best-laid plans.

Proper tactics begin with stance. The fighting stance, a fundamental concept of the martial arts, was directly influenced by the local terrain in which battle was fought and the type of enemy one expected to face. A proper stance could mean the difference between life and death and was designed to give the fighter stability, power, and strength in defense. A wide horse stance allowed him to maintain balance on uneven ground and avoid an attack by shifting his weight sideways. Consider the defensive posture of a judo practitioner, feet apart and body lowered by bending the knees, which prevents him from being unbalanced or thrown. Stances were further developed for fighting in enclosed areas which restricted the use of footwork and movement. If an attack could not be avoided through movement, the fighter could absorb the blow by bending his knees and sinking into a lower stance.[6]

Additionally, stance served a mental function by allowing the fighter to establish command presence. Displaying confidence through stance indicates physical and mental readiness and might give the martial artist the power to win by intimidation alone; thus, winning without fighting, which Sun Tzu prescribed as the best way to victory. If this is not possible, the Chinese classics advocate thwarting the attack rather than facing the adversary head-on.[7] Since successful warfare requires adaptation, however, a warrior must modify his stance to suit the circumstances of combat and his personal physical build. This is why some of the traditional stances seem less relevant to the modern martial artist participating, for example, in no-holds-barred combat relying on quick footwork and a mix of stand-up and ground fighting techniques.

Generally, the stances used in the Western martial arts vary less than those typically seen in the traditional Asian arts. A boxing stance places the fighter sideways, knees slightly bent, and with the dominant foot to the rear. Swordsmanship in the medieval era in Europe did not advocate any particular stance, but propagated the idea that the knight should use whatever footwork he found to be the most beneficial. Although a number of postures or guard positions were taught, rather than keeping one side of his body facing the opponent, the knight could strike with the sword equally well from a left or right stance, and would advance in an alternating stride to speed up movement and increase the reach and power of the attack. Balance and agility were still central to stance and, most importantly, a stance was not static.[8]

Ground, or the environment, is yet a crucial factor of war which guides the martial artist in his choice of strategy and stance. When Sun Tzu spoke about posture, his reasoning did not stop at the particular stance of the individual soldier, but extended to the strategic positioning of the army. The goal was to gain as much mobility and flexibility as possible. He listed six types of ground and how to fight on each. Some comprised long distances, others short; some were treacherous, others more secure. He called ground easy to reach but difficult to get out of entangling ground; its nature being such that one can easily defeat an enemy who is unprepared. Terrain equally disadvantageous to both belligerents he called temporizing. Such ground would prompt one to use deception by drawing the enemy forward and striking from a position of strength.[9] When studying stance, one might keep in mind that China has historically fought lengthy battles against nomadic warriors of considerable equestrian skill, who, because of their ability to live off the land, could mount swift attacks and disperse just as quickly.

Martial artists exploring the practicality of their techniques in difficult terrain. The Chinese martial arts use many stances that prove particularly suitable for wielding weapons. *(Image source: Aldhous, Wikimedia Commons)*

The terrain in which one fights can thus be a hindrance, but it can also be utilized to the martial artist's advantage if he has studied it in advance and is well schooled in its use. Clausewitz noted how the terrain offers several advantages, such as obstacles to the opponent's advance or the ability to check attacks to one's flanks. For example, if you find yourself in a multiple opponent scenario, a doorway may be used to check the enemy's advance or guard against attacks to your flanks or rear, because a large group of fighters cannot pass through a narrow opening at one time. In China, there is a saying: "With only one guarding the mountain pass, ten thousand men are not able to pass."[10] Thus, a single man does not need overwhelming physical strength to fight multiple opponents as long as he occupies advantageous terrain. In Western military history, the battle of Thermopylae in 480 BCE offers a revealing example of how a much stronger enemy can be stalled by a few men through the skillful use of terrain. A force of merely three hundred elite Spartan warriors fighting under King Leonidas I of Sparta, in addition to a few thousand Thespian, Theban, and other assistants

Using the environment to your advantage, for example, placing your back against the ropes can protect your rear and flanks, but it can also limit your mobility and cut off your escape routes. *(Image source: U.S. Military, Wikimedia Commons)*

were able to stall the Persian army fighting under the Persian Empire of Xerxes I, allegedly numbering in the millions (per Greek historian Herodotus of Halicarnassus). Only after the Spartans had suffered betrayal did the Persian army manage a breakthrough and ultimately surround and kill the Spartans to the last man.

Although many Asian martial arts seem shrouded in mysticism to the Western practitioner, Sun Tzu was a practical person who stressed the importance of seizing the initiative and shifting the balance of power in one's favor through the use of cunning and surprise. The deceptive army takes advantage of opportunities through swiftness and flexibility in movement and amasses full force against the critical point, ending the fight in minimum time and with as few losses as possible. Deception on the strategic level is based on good intelligence. How does the enemy think? What are his plans? What does he fear most? If you know his fears, you can capitalize on them and make him stage troops, for example, at an area he does not need to defend and that you do not intend to attack.

An enemy who believes that you will meet him in frontal assault will fail to guard his rear or flanks. Consider the Carthaginian general Hannibal Barca, who became famous for the deceptive pincer movement he used to defeat the numerically superior Roman army in the Battle of Cannae in 216 BCE. The maneuver relied on drawing the enemy into a trap and cutting off the escape routes. The reason why Hannibal Barca succeeded was because he created the illusion that his own forces were retreating by drawing back the center of the line, tempting the enemy to move forward. This maneuver allowed his relatively sparse forces to envelop the enemy and attack the flanks and rear where they were unprepared. But success depended on an opponent who was willing to engage in direct battle. Sun Tzu warned against trying this maneuver against an adversary who was prone to running. He even encouraged leaving the enemy an escape path because an army that is left with no way out, he argued, would fight to the death and cause great devastation in both armies: "For it is the nature of soldiers to resist when surrounded, to fight to the death when there is no alternative."[11]

Deceptive moves must be convincing in order to have value. In the martial arts, a broad shift in weight, for example, can create the illusion of forward or reverse movement and cause the opponent to move into the power of a strike. The drunken style kung-fu practitioner hides his intents by relying extensively on deceptive body movements, launching his strikes from unexpected angles and disrupting the opponent's concentration. (As Sun Tzu said, "A confused army leads to another's victory." [12]) Yet he stays in full control of his body by using the strength of his core (abdomen) to maintain balance. Drunken style kung-fu, which was popularized by actor Jackie Chan, has roots in many styles of traditional Chinese martial arts. It may have been created at the Shaolin Temple, "or by warriors posing as Shaolin monks who, no doubt, would often drink alcohol, and who later developed a system based on the emboldening qualities of alcohol."[13]

Capoeira, a Brazilian martial art founded several hundred years ago by African slaves, likewise relies extensively on deceptive and evasive body movements, with attacks focusing on leg sweeps and kicks from unusual positions. The practitioner of this art might appear to attempt a spinning leg sweep by dropping his bodyweight, but throws instead an unexpected spinning heel kick to his adversary's head. The art naturally requires great athletic ability. A skilled capoeira practitioner can reach tremendous speed in a spin kick and can easily knock his opponent unconscious. Small body size might actually benefit him because of the lower energy requirement of moving a small body and the greater ease with which he can gain speed in a spin kick. A fighter relying on a more direct approach to combat may beat a capoeira stylist by launching a strike when the opponent is in the middle of a complex maneuver such as a cartwheel. But such an act requires good timing. Timing is not about speed, strength, or superior physical build, but about the ability to strike a precise target when the opponent least expects it and preferably when he is moving into the strike's path of power. The consequence of taking a strike from a big fighter in possession of superb timing will be particularly devastating to the capoeira stylist because of the tremendous speed with which he moves his body. He might, in effect, knock himself out against the opponent's fist.

Good timing can also create sensory overload, a state of confusion and chaos often experienced by a fighter who is attacked repeatedly with explosive combinations. The concept of flow, as noted in chapter 1, is about avoiding a strike while remaining in position to strike the adversary. Thus, Sun Tzu's saying that "the momentum of one skilled in war is overwhelming, and his attack precisely timed."[14] Flow, a concept of deep importance in the Asian martial arts, further relates to rhythmic movement, the maintenance of proper distance in an engagement, and mental stability. "According to Far Eastern thinking, all of life is flow. You must learn to move and conduct your affairs in harmony with the universal scheme of things so you may master the art of living."[15] The Western world has adopted elements of flow along with the complementary opposites of yin and yang in modern warfare. A 1989 U.S. Marine Corps manual based on Clausewitz's teachings notes that combat is comprised of two essential components: fire and movement. These appear to represent opposite ends of the spectrum yet are mutually dependent. Movement allows one to exploit the effects of enemy fire. Simultaneously, firing at the enemy when on the offensive and moving increases the devastation of maneuver warfare.[16]

Although the strength of martial arts styles such as drunken style kung-fu and capoeira lies in the practitioner's ability to confuse the adversary, how the opponent carries himself and the use of little gestures and idiosyncrasies can tell you a lot about his strategy. Sun Tzu said, "If the enemy is far away and challenges you to do battle, he wants you to advance."[17] In a sparring match, you might interpret the opponent's enticing gesture or wave with his hand as cockiness, as an invitation to come closer and show him "what you've got." But his true intent is to unbalance you mentally and create a favorable opportunity for throwing a perfectly timed strike to your jaw and knock you out. According to Sun Tzu, the opponent would be engaging in good strategy, because all warfare is based on deception and one should "[h]old out baits to lure the enemy." The question for you is not so much about whether or not you will take the bait, but whether you can use good strategy to outwit the adversary. Sun Tzu also said that if the opponent "is arrogant, try to encourage his egotism."[18] If you decide to respond to his enticing gesture and move forward, be prepared for the trump card he has hidden in his sleeve. To thwart the attack, you must stay a step ahead in planning. You might try moving forward at a slight angle instead of straight in, maintaining a superior position away from his line of power.

Humility, in contrast to over-confidence, can also be used deceptively in the martial arts. When an argument is escalating and the situation is becoming hostile, you might try to bring the opponent's guard down by offering an apology and explaining that you do not want to fight. The idea is to "make the enemy see [your] strengths as weaknesses and [your] weaknesses as strengths."[19] But if he underestimates your intentions and is mentally underprepared, he will be taught a hard lesson when you reach out to shake his hand in friendly apology and instead grab his fingers in a brutal joint lock.

In Western martial arts that rely on the direct approach to battle, one can try deceiving the opponent by faking a strike to one area

If you are skilled at the ground game, it may benefit you to take the opponent down. You can increase your chances of victory by using techniques intended to deceive him prior to the takedown. *(Image source: The U.S. Army, Wikimedia Commons)*

and attacking another, or pretending to engage in a stand-up fight when the goal is a ground fight. Many fighters are head hunters. Try throwing multiple strikes to the opponent's head while pressing the attack. When you have trained him to defend his head, launch a roundhouse kick to his thigh area. Or better still if you are skilled at the ground game and he is not, shoot for his lower legs and take him down. You can also use deception within a move. Instead of standing toe-to-toe with the opponent and counterstriking, drop to the ground the moment he lands a strike to your body to create the impression that his strike did damage. As Sun Tzu said, simulate disorder where there is order. Simultaneously grab his legs and take him to the ground with you.

Yet a way to enjoy a relative strength advantage is by dividing the enemy forces. Sun Tzu's saying, "The place of battle must not be made known to the enemy,"[20] demonstrates the importance of splitting the hostile force. By not announcing one's intentions, one can compel the enemy to defend many places simultaneously, preventing him from consolidating his strength against the critical point:

> If I am able to determine the enemy's dispositions while,
> at the same time, I conceal my own, then I can concen-
> trate my forces and his must be divided. And if I con-
> centrate while he divides, I can use my entire strength
> to attack a fraction of his. Therefore, I will be numeri-
> cally superior.[21]

A strategy focusing on dividing the enemy forces enables the
martial artist to appear superior when he is inferior in stature or
strength. Sun Tzu and Clausewitz agreed that the best way to accomplish this is by attacking the opponent's center of gravity; his
balance point, because this will naturally split his forces and ability
to counterattack.[22] A practitioner of drunken kung-fu excels at evasive tactics and has naturally trained to achieve superb balance particularly in unusual postures. If you were to fight this martial artist,
how would you go about attacking his center of gravity? Although
Sun Tzu and Clausewitz agreed that defense is the stronger form of
war (as will be discussed in greater detail in chapter 7) in the sense
that the defensive position requires less energy expenditure and
therefore benefits the weaker army, they clearly understood that
defense is only viable if used as a springboard for offense. Although
you can deter an attack for some time and wait for the most opportune moment to counterattack, you cannot win a fight through
defense alone. You will defeat a person who is master at evasion by
preventing him from evading your attack, for example, by corner-
ing him or luring him into close range. The fact that evasion works
best from long range reinforces the importance of knowing the terrain. When fighting a drunken style kung-fu practitioner, if possible,
choose an arena that does not give him the space he needs to execute evasive movement. Likewise, if your opponent is an exceptionally strong long range kicker, try attacking his center of gravity
from close range where he cannot use a kick against you. Or take
his ground and destroy his foundation with kicks to his legs.

The traditional martial arts are not so much about body size and
physical strength as about the ability to deliver the greatest impact
to the target in the shortest amount of time, or what Sun Tzu re-

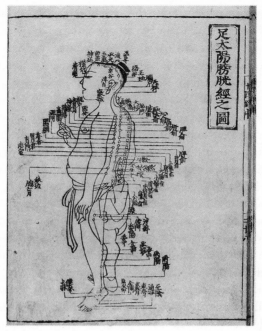

Early Ming Dynasty meridian chart from Hua Shou (acupuncture). The concept of *dim mak*, or the death touch, might have originated in Chinese medicine. A complete understanding of the human body's weaknesses and strengths would potentially allow a skilled martial artist to strike a pressure point, split and conquer the opposing force, and defeat a stronger adversary. *(Image source: Wikimedia Commons)*

ferred to as consolidation of strength against the critical point, and which demonstrates the pragmatic approach he took to warfare. Precise blows to vulnerable targets such as nerve centers have the capacity to split the opposing forces and momentarily paralyze the adversary or even end the fight. A precise strike to a nerve center on the forearm, for example, can get a knife-wielding adversary to drop his weapon instantly.

Other options for splitting the hostile force involve decreasing the opponent's defensive capability by attacking separate targets in rapid succession. For example, strike to the head and then kick to the legs. When his focus shifts to defending his legs, move in and elbow him in the face. Then drop your weight, grab his legs, and take his foundation. The practitioner of mixed martial arts tends to view the opponent's whole body as a target: the ankles, legs, torso, arms, wrists, neck, and head. He must be in exceptional physical shape when fighting others of the same discipline, and must have enough understanding of human anatomy to know which targets are the most vulnerable and deserve the greatest protection. For example, he must keep his guard up to protect his head and his chin down to protect his neck and throat. He must keep his elbows tight to his body to protect his ribs and kidneys. And he must avoid inadvertently extending his arms toward the adversary to protect his elbows and wrists.

One can also split the hostile force by attacking multiple times to the same target such as the head or outer thigh area, and create sensory overload, preventing the opponent from counterstriking. A sustained effort in firepower, or the continuous bombardment of the adversary, will force him to focus on defense, may unbalance him, and will generally cause chaos and disorientation. The moment he extends his arm to counter, he will expose a vulnerable target. When related to the sport aspects of the fighting arts, a competitor can gain points by demonstrating to the judges that he has the capacity to dominate the fight through a number of successive blows.

An important ingredient in Clausewitz's theory of war is fighting a decisive battle. In other words, the battle has to lead to a decision; it is a means to an end rather than an end in itself, with each blow bringing you a step closer to the objective. Although decisive battle implies pitting strength against strength in accord with the armies of ancient Greece and Rome, within the decisive battle are elements of movement and deception designed to weaken a superior enemy. Movement, as a part of strategy, does not concern itself directly with the use of military forces in combat, but with the object of war. The purpose is to position so that one can better utilize the tactics at one's disposal, press the attack, and destroy the enemy forces.

In order to fully utilize movement and truly benefit from surprise, however, one must attack where the enemy is unprepared.

This requires the indirect approach to warfare and the ability to hold the initiative. Furthermore, surprise may not be possible if you are the defender, for example, in a street fight or home robbery. On the strategic level, the successful use of surprise gives you a relative strength advantage and increases your fighting spirit. While the element of surprise is invaluable for gaining a strategic advantage that assists an army in amassing power against the decisive point, Clausewitz acknowledged that deception is difficult to use with success. The army must also be ready to act rapidly once surprise is achieved.

While strategy requires sufficient planning that can inadvertently be revealed to the enemy prior to the fight, tactics happen at the spur of the moment and limit the adversary's ability to predict which move to defend against next. The fact that warfare in Clausewitz's time was waged with modern equipment in mass armies, with access to long range weapons and firepower, might be a reason why he did not emphasize deception on the strategic level like Sun Tzu did, but considered it principally an element of tactics. "[S]urprise lies at the root of all operations without exception," he suggested, "though in widely varying degrees depending on the nature and circumstances of the operation."[23] However, he recognized that what surprise gains on the tactical level in the form of "easy execution, it loses in the efficacy," because "the greater the efficacy the greater always the difficulty of execution." Ultimately, good tactics lead to victory, but you will generally not achieve great results with a small surprise on the tactical level or score complete victory with a single tactical move.[24]

Unlike Sun Tzu, Clausewitz also made a clear distinction between strategic defense and strategic offense. If somebody breaks into your home and you defend yourself by harming or killing the adversary, you are on the strategic defensive no matter how aggressive your conduct. The person instigating the fight by attempting to rob you is on the strategic offensive, even if he is unable to do you harm. This is one reason why the martial artist can legitimately employ ruthless techniques aimed to maim or kill the adversary while claiming to engage in defense and not offense. Although holding back a strategic reserve is senseless because the war can be lost in the first battle, the object should be to minimize losses until you find an opportunity to turn the situation to your advantage. By contrast, holding back a tactical reserve (conserving your energy) is vital to success.[25]

Finally, the social, political, and economic conditions of a state (or individual fighter) must be considered when determining strategy, because these conditions often influence motivation and initiative. Clausewitz's famous dictum that war is simply a continuation of policy (political intercourse) by other means suggests in part that people relate to each other through violence, and war (or combat) is the means or instrument by which one furthers one's political aim. Consider a person getting robbed at gun point. Should he hand over the wallet and car keys and be thankful that he managed to escape with his life intact? Or should he play hardball and offer the robber some snotty comment in return for the intrusion? What if he has just completed a course in haganah, an Israeli street fighting system that drills students in practical gun disarming techniques and other methods of self-defense? How does it change his leverage in this particular "political" situation?

A strategy that is successful in one battle may not be similarly successful in another under a different set of social and political circumstances. Ideally, a skilled martial artist considers the mentality, intelligence, will, emotions, and other psychological factors of each potential belligerent. He or she is aware of the full "political" situation, is able to discriminate and make wise choices, and knows exactly how much he can achieve on his road to victory with the means at his disposal. Ultimately, however, he cannot escape the uncertainty of battle and the crippling effects of friction.

CHAPTER 5

IMPOSING YOUR WILL

"Therefore the clever combatant imposes his will on the enemy, but does not allow the enemy's will to be imposed on him."   — Sun Tzu

"War is an act of force to compel our enemy to do our will."   — Carl von Clausewitz

To win a fight, you must convince the opponent of your motives. When all hope of compromise or otherwise peaceful settlement has fallen by the wayside, you make him submit to your will by incapacitating him physically or defeating him mentally. Imposing your will on the enemy is at the core about seizing the initiative. As Sun Tzu stated, "those skilled in war bring the enemy to the field of battle and are not brought there by him."[1] Carl von Clausewitz agreed by noting that war is a struggle for power. He differed from Sun Tzu mainly in his view that war must involve a physical exchange of blows and cannot be resolved by diplomatic means, or else it is not war: The presumption is "that the enemy [will] not accept [your] will without a fight, for if he [does] there [will] be no war."[2] Although battle is a trial of physical strength and stamina and Clausewitz underscored the importance of attacking the enemy with concentrated force, he understood that one can also defeat him by breaking his spirit. For example, if the enemy's center of gravity is his mental strength, breaking him mentally through a convincing display of power will defeat him even as his physical forces remain intact. Note that the threat of a physical engagement must be realistic.

However, the best way to compel the enemy to do your will may be by disarming him; by taking away his weapons, be it a knife, stick, or gun; by damaging a limb or joint; or by taking his balance so that he cannot retaliate even as he retains the use of his weapons. Although the objective, to defeat the adversary by imposing your will on him, remains constant, the means by which you achieve it may vary. A krav maga practitioner, for example, might block an attack and throw a crippling strike to the adversary's throat while moving to close range before disarming him with a joint lock. A hapkido or taekwondo practitioner might choose to eliminate a weapon with a well-placed powerful kick to the adversary's arm. Either way, if the disarming technique succeeds, the adversary will be at your mercy and experience a crippling feeling of dismay when realizing that his weapon is gone and he is physically incapacitated.

Many traditional Asian martial arts are both dynamic and brutal in the execution of technique, giving the practitioner a tremendous capacity to impose his will on the adversary. In the many variations of karate, victory often comes by relentlessly bombarding the opponent with strikes and kicks, by knocking him out, by rendering him incapable of continued fighting, or in sports competition, by scoring points. The softer styles of martial arts are no less brutal and undermine the opponent's fighting spirit through the principle of nonresistance, seizing his strength and using it against him by responding to an opportunity as it appears rather than seeking it out. Practitioners of judo, for example, attack the adversary's balance through dynamic throws, destroying his capacity to defend and counterattack. Waiting until the adversary grabs some part of your body (shoulder, neck, wrist) further provides an opportunity for creating a stable foundation from which to initiate a lock against his elbow, wrist, or fingers.

Submission fighting on the ground likewise relies on nonresistance to impose one's will on the adversary and convince him to acknowledge defeat. Choke holds, arm bars, and leg locks are applied as the opportunity arises. An opponent on his back will almost always expose his elbow and give you an arm bar; an opponent on his side or belly will give you a choke hold; an opponent straddling you will give you a finger lock the moment he exposes his hand to grab or strike you. Your goal remains constant throughout the scenario: to defeat the adversary by imposing your will on him.[3] In real-life events, one can also win by some intermediate action, for example, by placing the adversary in a position where he would choose to give up or negotiate a settlement rather than fight. Thus, it is possible to obtain the objective merely through a display of power and the resolve to fight.

Although Sun Tzu and Clausewitz differed slightly in their definition of war, they agreed that the army's strength should be preserved and victory secured in the quickest way possible. This chapter examines several Asian and European fighting styles, demonstrating how fighters from ancient to modern times have succeeded in combat by seizing the initiative, pressing the attack, and imposing their will on the adversary often through physically damaging blows, but also through the destruction of the opponent's fighting spirit.

Key Points: Imposing Your Will

Sun Tzu	Carl von Clausewitz
Imposing your will on the enemy means seizing the initiative through minimum energy expenditure.	War is a struggle for power that involves physical force. The best way to impose your will on the adversary is by disarming him.
Secure victory in the quickest way possible by undermining the enemy's fighting spirit.	If you cannot break your opponent physically, then break his spirit.
Use tactics wisely to weaken the opponent's resistance and shift the battle in your favor.	Seek a quick end to battle by concentrating the forces against the decisive point.

Shock the enemy into submission through sudden bursts of energy and by relentlessly pressing the attack.

Create a state of instability in the opposing force through continuous offensive action.

Imposing your will on the adversary may at first seem contradictory to the message of traditional martial arts. As can be argued, the brutality involved in pressing the attack creates a sense of tunnel vision or blindness to adaptation, where lack of personal expression prevents the practitioner from utilizing the proven concepts of flow, yin and yang, and yielding to the opponent's power. But, as demonstrated in previous chapters, the martial arts are historically about combat. And combat is at the core about winning, regardless of whether it takes place in Asia, Europe, or the United States.

Wrestling, the forerunner to modern submission fighting, is an ancient martial art several thousand years old, and may be the earliest combat style practiced in all parts of the world with the intent

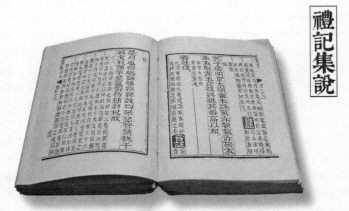

The practice of jiao li, one of the oldest Chinese grappling arts dating to the Zhou Dynasty (c. 1050-256 BCE), was recorded in the Classic of Rites of the Confucian body of rules describing social forms, governmental systems, and ceremonial rites. The fighting art, developed for use by soldiers, encompassed strikes, joint locks, throws, and pressure point attacks. It eventually became a popular sport in ancient China with the most skilled practitioners promoted to bodyguards for the emperor. *(Image source: Wikimedia Commons)*

of imposing one's will on the adversary. In China, wrestling "was known as *kakhio* or *koryohi*, meaning 'Korean sport.'" Murals of an ancient stone chamber in Manchuria portray wrestling scenes, and the *Li-chiyueh-ling*, an old Chinese book, records that wrestling contests were ordered by the emperor for the troops in midwinter to toughen them. Japan, too, has a history of wrestling. Sumo relies on size and strength over finesse with the goal of unbalancing a lighter or less skilled opponent and forcing him out of the ring.[4] In the West, wrestlers using techniques nearly identical to those used by modern practitioners are depicted in cave art several thousand years old. Wrestling was popularized in the Olympic Games of the ancient Greeks.

The striking arts likewise enjoy a long history of imposing one's will on the adversary. The *Bubishi* (see also Wu Bei Zhi), or *Account of Military Arts and Science*, a two-part Chinese document dating to the late Ming Dynasty (1366-1644 CE) for the first book and middle to late Qing Dynasty (1644-1911 CE) for the second, is one of the earliest texts about karate that demonstrates techniques designed to destroy an adversary's fighting spirit, not necessarily through crushing blows (although these are pictured in abundance as well), but through leg takedowns, body throws, and strikes aimed at typically nonlethal targets.[5] This massive book compiled for the purpose of restoring the physical condition of the military forces in China, discusses tactics for close quarter armed and unarmed combat, illustrating how to impose one's will on the adversary by attacking a weakness in his anatomy.[6]

Joints, for example, are critical targets that offer opportunities for control. Grabbing the adversary's arm while simultaneously striking with a palm to his jaw might enable the practitioner to proceed with a takedown through the use of a weak link in the body: the neck. Grabbing his jaw and tilting his head back and to the side through its full range of motion, or pulling his hair while pushing against his chin, can be used as options for the neck takedown and affords one control of the adversary by destroying his ability to resist or retaliate. Hyper-extending the opponent's elbow by placing his straight arm across your shoulder gives you leverage to damage this joint using relatively little force. Although hyper-extension does not result in death, it will likely destroy the opponent's weapons and zap him of his fighting spirit.

Practitioners of predominant kicking arts such as taekwondo impose their will on the adversary, for example, by setting up a kick to the jaw with a series of hand techniques, forcing the opponent to corner himself with his back to the ropes. The flexibility in the legs of a skilled taekwondo practitioner enables him to throw high kicks with accuracy also from very close range and score a victory. A taekwondo fighter might capitalize on these strengths when fighting an adversary who favors punches or low kicks, such as a Muay Thai boxer. Simultaneously, he must prevent the opponent from gaining a positional advantage or capitalizing on the typical strengths of the Thai boxer: leg kicks, knees, and throws.

Western martial arts likewise emphasize controlling the adversary and breaking his spirit through the use of overwhelming force coupled with relentless attack. Boxing has a history that stretches several thousand years and can be traced through pictorial evidence. The boxer seizes the initiative and presses the attack with brutal offense aimed at wearing the enemy down and forcing him to retreat. Furthermore, the boxer who controls the environment or ring area through footwork and the use of good tactics, generally controls the fight and will score favorably with the judges. Boxing great Muhammad Ali's famous saying, "Float like a butterfly, sting like a bee," certainly carries weight.

Several options thus exist for imposing one's will on the adversary: You may harm him physically, frighten him into submission, or convince him that the battle is not worth fighting. Simultaneously, the opponent will strive to impose his will on you. Many of Sun Tzu's principles rely on the use of good tactics to shift the battle in your favor. If you cannot defeat the adversary outright, you must weaken his resistance by attacking targets intended to cause extreme pain or incapacitation. Joint locks are perhaps particularly useful for splitting his focus. The sudden and intense pain inflicted by a joint lock applied with accuracy and determination will quickly bring an adversary to his knees.

Depiction of Minoan youths boxing, from the Minoan civilization that arose on the island of Crete c. 2700-1500 BCE, and the earliest documented use of gloves for training purposes. *(Image source: Marsyas, Wikimedia Commons)*

Hapkido, a combination of several martial principles and an art that offers an arsenal of pain compliance techniques, can break bones and damage ligaments but will not necessarily kill the adversary outright. The hapkido practitioner seizes the initiative by blocking the opponent's attack, simultaneously moving to close range while exerting forward pressure and striking to a target intended to shock the adversary, split his focus, and wear him down physically and mentally. A good option is a knee strike to the groin or midsection. Defense and offense are viewed as parts of the same technique. Since one cannot win a fight through defense alone, as will be discussed in chapter 7, the counterattack must come the moment the opponent is stunned by a block, parry, or evasive move. Practitioners of hapkido rely on the water principle, as discussed in chapter 1. Like water, which finds its way through any crevice and can wear down the toughest materials given enough time, the hapkido practitioner focuses on penetrating the target rather than snapping a strike or kick back to the point of origin, or if this is not possible, penetrating the opponent's defenses.

Yet a way to impose one's will on the adversary is by sabotaging the power of his techniques by manipulating his balance. The takedowns and throws of hapkido rely on leverage and can end a fight instantly, or at least damage the adversary's fighting spirit, giving the practitioner the mental edge he needs to win. The moment you catch or grab the adversary's leg, drive forward, or sweep his supporting foot, his main concern is retaining his balance rather than counterstriking. Strikes to the ribs, abdomen, or groin will momentarily weaken him in preparation for the takedown. Furthermore, forcing the enemy to retreat swings the odds in your favor.

Speed and courage are naturally critical elements that must be part of the fighter's repertoire. Hsing-i chuan, an internal martial art of Northern China, although practiced mainly for health, offers a good example of how to strengthen the body and build proper spirit for imposing one's will on an adversary. Based on only five basic strategic moving patterns, hsing-i chuan was developed to help soldiers gain combat proficiency quickly. The empty hand and weapon techniques (saber and bayonet) of hsing-i chuan were taught to the officers at the Central Military Academy at Nanjing during the Second Sino-Japanese War (1937-1945 CE) in an attempt to adapt a traditional Chinese martial art to modern warfare. However, a number of masters had proposed teaching the techniques of hsing-i chuan to soldiers in preparation for combat several decades earlier. The style also became popular because of its success in the national martial arts competition held in Nanjing in 1928.[7]

The hsing-i chuan practitioner imposes his will on the enemy through coordinated movements coupled with sudden bursts of energy, through linear footwork and pressing the attack. The ideology behind the art is to shock the enemy into submission and end the fight as quickly as if you were thrusting a spear through him. The elbows are kept close to the body to facility power and speed. As Sun Tzu reminded us, when the flanks are exposed and in trouble, you need to bring the forces back to the center in order to protect yourself and preserve strength for a renewed attack.[8]

Although performed in linear fashion along the centerline of the body, the moves of hsing-i chuan follow a vertical circular pattern that promotes speed and deception. For example, the practitioner may deflect a strike by bringing his arm straight up along his centerline, grabbing the opponent's wrist and pulling him forward to negate his balance. He may also use a downward parry to the opponent's arm, simultaneously throwing a palm strike with his other hand to the jaw, all the while pressing the attack. Offense occurs almost simultaneously with defense, making the art time efficient. Kicks may be blocked through a violent downward slap with both hands to the opponent's leg, followed by a small step forward and a strike to the head to shock his system. The enemy is thus pursued and exploited through continuous aggressive action that will deprive him of an opportunity to regroup his strategy or replenish his forces.

Two concepts in particular make hsing-i chuan an effective fighting art: the division of the hostile force and flow, which entails the ability to meet the opponent's attack and counterstrike within a defensive move. Both Sun Tzu and Clausewitz recognized the importance of the principle of continuity. As noted by Sun Tzu, "When torrential water tosses boulders, it is because of its momentum . . .

Thus the momentum of one skilled in war is overwhelming, and his attack precisely regulated."[9] Although stressing that ideal war differs from the reality, Clausewitz agreed that continuous action opens the way to victory. In fact, "suspension of action in war is a contradiction of terms," because two armies, "like fire and water, never find themselves in a state of equilibrium."[10] Offensive action will thus dominate on the side that is more strongly motivated to impose his will on the other.

As an aggressive combat art, hsing-i chuan permits no evasive moves prior to counterattack. Many techniques occur at very close range. However, pressing the attack is not synonymous with chasing the opponent. Rather, the hsing-i chuan practitioner waits for the opponent to initiate a move which he then intercepts, defending and counterstriking simultaneous to forward movement. He further divides the enemy's balance line and attacks his structural base by checking his leg, weakening his stance, and promoting a continuous offensive flow of strikes, grabs, or takedowns. Kicks are generally thrown to low targets. The moment the enemy regains his composure, he is already defeated.

Wing chun kung-fu, popularized by Yip Man (1893-1972 CE) and Bruce Lee (1940-1973 CE) in the early 1960s, is yet an art based on short range combat and forward pressure. Battle is won by dominating the opponent's space, imposing one's will on him by smothering him with punches and kicks. Much like firing an automatic weapon, the relentless bombardment of the same target—the solar plexus, chest, or head—will overwhelm the adversary, force him to retreat, and rob him of his fighting spirit. Centerline power, keeping your arms within the boundaries of your body and avoiding overextension, relates to Clausewitz's emphasis on seeking a quick end to battle by concentrating the forces against the decisive point, giving the enemy no time to reset his balance or regain his composure. The drawback of continuous fast punching is the exceptional endurance required for a sustained effort. Success demands aggression and an ability to stay a step ahead of the adversary. Rather than retreating to avoid a blow, the wing chun practitioner intercepts it and presses forward with continuous rapid-fire strikes, his first counterstrike ideally landing on target the moment he blocks the opponent's attack.

Since wing chun is an in-your-face close combat style, kicks must be set up with punches. Once at close range, kicks can be thrown deceptively to low targets such as the knees. Front kicks to the body are also used to stop an enemy's advance. A properly timed kick to the body can do significant damage or knock the opponent off balance. Many wing chun techniques focus on controlling the opponent by tying up his arms so that he is physically unable to retaliate or defend himself. Wing chun master Lo Man Kam says that wing chun "focuses more on agility and skill rather than brute force, and is first and foremost about protecting yourself."[11] However, the style was developed for use on the streets where winning in the quickest way possible proves crucial. When the fight is over, there should be no question as to who is the winner.

The hybrid martial arts likewise offer some good examples of how to seize the initiative, press the attack, and impose one's will on the adversary. Kajukenbo, founded in Hawaii in 1947, as indicated in its name is derived from karate (ka), judo or jujutsu (ju), kenpo (ken), and Chinese boxing (bo). The kajukenbo fighter imposes his will on the adversary by striking to vital targets, making the enemy ripe for a takedown.[12] A martial artist well-versed in kajukenbo might intercept a strike and move forward with aggressive offense, forcing the adversary to retreat and taking him to the ground at the first opportune moment. If forced to go down with the opponent, he can resort to the techniques of jujutsu and compel the adversary to submit, for example, by applying an arm bar.

Among the European fighting styles, bartitsu offers an interesting example of a hybrid martial art. Developed in England in the late nineteen century, bartitsu is a precursor to the mixed martial arts. After returning from Asia, its founder, British entrepreneur Edward William Barton-Wright, named the art by combining the first part of his last name and jujutsu; thus, *bart-itsu*. By using his knowledge of Asian and Western martial arts, Barton-Wright attempted to create a comprehensive system of street defense that allowed the practitioner to seize the initiative and impose his will on the adversary without adhering to the typical Western ideal of pitting strength against strength. Bartitsu draws its techniques from boxing, judo, and jujutsu. It incorporates a variety of combat rang-

Bartitsu, a street defense style of martial art designed for the gentleman of Western society, incorporates common items of carry such as the walking stick to inflict damage on an adversary. *(Image source: Artful Dodger, Wikimedia Commons)*

es and also includes a number of stick techniques. For example, the bartitsu fighter might start by parrying an attack and moving to close range to upset the opponent's balance, and then attack a joint, such as the wrist, elbow, shoulder, knee, or neck to inflict pain and further damage the opponent's ability to counterattack. Strikes and kicks are used to close the distance between fighters and prepare for balance manipulation and joint lock techniques, and to split the opponent's focus and thus preventing him from regaining his composure. A walking stick carried by gentlemen is typically used to inflict further damage or defend against an opponent armed with a knife or stick.

The practitioner of bartitsu fights to the finish until the opponent can no longer use his weapons in offense or defense. He moves inside of a stick-wielding adversary's power and controls the fight from close range, breaking his enemy's focus and seizing the initiative by using unexpected techniques. Barton-Wright wrote:

> It is to meet eventualities of this kind, where a person is confronted suddenly in an unexpected way, that I have introduced a new style of self-defence, which can be very terrible in the hands of a quick and confident exponent. One of its greatest advantages is that the exponent need not necessarily be a strong man, or in training, or even a specially active man in order to paralyse a very formidable opponent, and it is equally applicable to a man who attacks you with a knife, or a stick, or against a boxer; in fact, it can be considered a class of self-defence designed to meet every possible kind of attack, whether armed or otherwise.[13]

Since many martial arts were developed for use on the streets, it is prudent to ask how to press the attack and seize the initiative when a weapon is involved. As mentioned previously, Clausewitz believed that the best way to impose your will on the adversary is by disarming him. Eskrima, a Filipino fighting style, may be of particular interest in this regard. The skilled eskrima fighter not only controls the weapon but takes the enemy down, preventing him from counterattacking. Eskrima has a recorded history that reaches to the early sixteenth century CE, when Portuguese explorer Ferdinand Magellan (1480-1521 CE) was killed in the Philippines by opponents wielding spears and other weapons. However, the art was likely used several hundred years prior to this incident in inter-tribal wars and against invading peoples. The weapons, typically sticks, are employed in strikes and as leverage against joints such as the elbow or wrist to control and disarm the adversary.

Like other arts that emphasize imposing one's will on the enemy, eskrima advocates seizing the initiative the moment the opponent strikes or grabs you rather than evading the attack. It is generally understood that a weapon is most dangerous when in motion, and to control it you must know where it is. Moving to close range and grabbing or pinning the adversary's weapon-wielding arm gives you a stationary point of reference that allows you to proceed with a disarming technique followed by a joint break or other damaging blow. Several possibilities exist. Landing a hard blow when engaged in a stick fight against a stick-wielding opponent will undoubtedly affect him mentally. Striking his weapon hand or striking a target on his body will split his focus and weaken his resistance. Blocking his weapon-wielding arm gives you an opportunity to disarm him through leverage, using the short end of the stick to pry the weapon from his hand. Any number of wrist locks can

Eskrima, a traditional martial art of the Philippines, uses weapons, mainly sticks, in offense and defense against an armed opponent. The skilled eskrima practitioner can use a variety of strikes and leverage techniques to impose his will on the adversary by inflicting pain or disarming him. (*Image source: Jonathan Makiling Abaya, Wikimedia Commons*)

also prove effective. A skilled eskrima fighter understands the weaknesses of the human anatomy and can loosen an adversary's grip by striking or twisting his wrist.

In contrast to the Asian martial arts, the Western way of war has historically emphasized imposing one's will on the adversary through direct attack and superior strength; although, several variations exist that tend to benefit the smaller martial artist. The Israeli art of krav maga (contact combat), considered one of the most efficient and devastating close combat fighting styles developed in modern times and taught to every new recruit in the IDF (Israeli Defense Forces), demonstrates the importance of keeping one's body in motion, pressing the attack, and overwhelming the enemy with a series of damaging blows. As a combination of several fighting styles, krav maga is constantly refined and updated in accord with changing enemy tactics and strategy. The art encompasses karate and Muay Thai strikes and blocks, judo throws, and a variety of grappling techniques. As a military combat art, it excels at disarming an adversary wielding a gun or knife. Although developed for use by the military, civilians currently enjoy learning krav maga, which is unique because it has no rules that limit what the practitioner can or cannot do, and no rankings (although some schools deviate from this tradition and award belts).

Krav maga, which does not adhere to an esoteric philosophy but was developed only for the reality of the battlefield and the street, aims at making effective fighters within three to six months of training. Used by law enforcement and the military, its purpose is to protect against danger by harming the adversary and taking away his will to fight. The underlying principle that a long war is costly teaches the krav maga practitioner to eliminate the threat in the quickest way possible. The victorious fighter seizes the initiative and meets the opponent's attack the moment he senses a threat. Timidity has no place in krav maga. When the adversary attacks with a knife, your goal is to intercept the attack, using forward momentum to strike, disarm, and take him down. The krav maga practitioner is taught to use the strength in his legs and drive his body forward into the opponent to stall his advance and upset his mental balance.

You can weaken him further by kneeing him in the groin. Note the similarity to hsing-i chuan which also relies on linear forward movement, repelling the adversary through nearly simultaneous defense and offense.

Blocking the attack is preferred over evasion in krav maga, because the physical contact gives the practitioner a point of reference from which to continue. In other words, you will know exactly where your opponent's weapon is, be it a knife, gun, or fist. Moving forward into disarming range can potentially shorten the duration of the fight. While an evasive move to the rear would prompt you to reset your balance before proceeding with offense, aggressive forward pressure allows you to use momentum to seize and retain the initiative. The spirit is never to give up. Naturally you need very good endurance to press the attack and throw continuous strikes until the enemy is neutralized. However, practitioners of krav maga rely on the intensity and severity of the techniques to end the fight quickly.

Russian sambo (unarmed self-defense) is yet a violent and practical Western martial art which purpose it is to control the adversary by imposing your will on him, and which, unlike krav maga, requires exceptional technical expertise. Developed in the pre-World War II years and the precursor to the mixed martial arts fought in the octagon, it is a modern descendent of Russia's bloody war history. Evolved from military combat, sambo saw great success in early competitions against judoka. Its many unorthodox techniques used with full intent of ending the fight quickly made it a versatile fighting art and true test of physical and mental tenacity.

Sambo encompasses karate style strikes and kicks, judo style takedowns and throws, and jujutsu style arm and leg locks. Used by the elite units of the Red Army, by bodyguards and police squads, it requires a well-rounded fighter in excellent physical condition. The bodyguard often has no time to draw his weapon and must react instantly with an empty hand technique to disarm the adversary and neutralize the threat. Many of the techniques involve breaking the opponent's balance while controlling the weapon hand, for example, by kicking or sweeping the opponent's leg or applying a neck takedown.

Success in sambo naturally requires close range fighting skills, particularly when a firearm is involved. The sambo practitioner might avoid the line of fire by parrying the weapon hand and force-fully grabbing the adversary's wrist, controlling the arm and the gun, and splitting the adversary's focus, taking him off balance with a stunning strike to the head. A bodyguard or police officer would not have as his goal to kill the enemy, yet must demonstrate total control of the fight. He imposes his will by destroying the adver-sary's physical capacity to continue the fight, for example, through a joint lock or break. Every move has to count. A sidekick to the opponent's ribs is not used as a distraction to set up another strike, but is aimed at ending the fight and must have the full weight of the body behind it. It will at the very least knock the opponent back and probably break his ribs. Kicking and simultaneously grab-bing the opponent's arm is particularly devastating because it allows the sambo practitioner to use his adversary's body as leverage, pull-ing him forward while delivering the kick with maximum power.[14]

In addition to physically incapacitating the enemy, imposing your will on him is about controlling his mind, his fighting spirit. Ultimately, the objective is to render him incapable of continued fighting. As seen time and again in Brazilian Jiu-jitsu, when an ad-versary becomes more concerned with his own survival than with your defeat, you have succeeded at imposing your will on him. Al-though a tough fighter will struggle against a choke or joint lock, he will know beyond a shadow of a doubt when he has lost the battle and must submit. The grappling arts are particularly useful for gain-ing intimate knowledge of what it takes to impose one's will on the enemy. Techniques that would kill in real life can be applied in the training hall gradually without doing one's training partner lasting harm, giving him the option of deciding when the battle is over. In Brazilian Jiu-jitsu and the many variant forms of grappling, there is no defeat unless the opponent signals defeat. This concept is important, because a fighter who admits to defeat has historically been less likely to take up the fight anew.

A superb athlete with an impressive physical build may further exercise his will over the adversary and win a fight through intimidation and command presence, making the enemy succumb to his reputation alone. The purpose of strategy, as discussed in chapter 4, is to break the enemy's resistance before the physical engagement. The stare-down that takes place before a boxing match, the *Wai Kru* prefight dance of the Muay Thai fighter, and even the meditation of a karateka are ways in which a fighter attempts to defeat his opponent psychologically before battle has begun.

How do you prevent the enemy from imposing his will on you? As suggested by practitioners of hsing-i chuan, one way is by conserving energy and cultivating fighting spirit.[15] Preventing the enemy from capitalizing on his strengths or presenting a counter-threat might also compel a potential attacker to abandon the fight altogether. According to Sun Tzu, the skillful fighter retains the initiative by entering a fight on his own terms and placing the enemy on unfavorable ground. We realize, of course, that this is an idealistic statement that is not always possible to act upon. But

Composure and a silent display of power can be psychological weapons aimed at breaking the opponent's fighting spirit. *(Image source: Nickolay Shiryaev, Wikimedia Commons)*

sufficient planning and preparation, as discussed in chapter 3, will bring the odds in your favor.

As demonstrated through the examples provided in this chapter, and as acknowledged by Sun Tzu and Clausewitz, battle is a struggle of will. Yet neither strategist favored prolonged conflict. The idea is always to expend as little effort as possible and win in the shortest amount of time by attacking the opponent's center of gravity, his critical vulnerability.

CHAPTER 6

DESTROYING THE
ENEMY FORCE

"He who understands how to fight in accordance with
the strength of antagonistic forces will be victorious."
— **Sun Tzu**

"All war supposes human weakness, and against that it
is directed." — **Carl von Clausewitz**

Battle should be entered from a position of strength (physical size,
muscular strength, well fed and rested, and with good morale and
courage). In offense and defense, the techniques the martial artist
uses should inflict damage that ultimately leads to the destruction
of the opposing force. In accordance with Sun Tzu's analogy, "The
army will be like throwing a stone against an egg,"[1] a strike or kick
should be aimed at a target that is inherently weak, such as the eyes,
throat, or groin. Using a strong weapon to defend against a weaker
weapon, for example, by jamming the elbow into an adversary's front
or roundhouse kick rather than blocking with the hand or forearm
allows the martial artist to practice this concept also in defense.

Ancient Chinese military writings speak of how victory should
come quickly, because the longer the military experience the greater the risk of disaster. Failing to destroy the opposing force can give
the enemy the power to rise again even if the initial attack proved

successful. Destructive capabilities are further increased by taking advantage of opportune moments in the fight and preventing the opponent from counterstriking, or as Sun Tzu reminded us, "When the enemy presents an opportunity, speedily take advantage of it."[2] His work on maneuver warfare illustrates the importance of positioning for proper use of strength. A speedy attack against the enemy's flanks or rear has potentially greater destructive capability than a head-on clash with the opposing force. If possible, do not allow an enemy to get behind you or to your weak side: "After crossing swamps and wetlands, strive to quickly get through them, and do not linger," position so that you have "dangerous ground in front, and safe ground to the back."[3]

Superior positioning is good strategy for any fighter, but particularly for he who is physically weaker or numerically inferior to the opponent. Superior positioning enables the martial artist to take the enemy by surprise, using speed and aggression when aiming for the total destruction of his forces. While meeting the enemy in direct attack can gain one access to centerline targets such as the groin, solar plexus, and throat, he who positions away from the enemy's line of power generally enjoys a relative strength advantage without risking immediate retaliation. Positioning to the side, for example, opens up targets to his outside thigh area and knee, kidney, and jaw. The relative superiority of a physically stronger opponent can thus be compromised by forcing him to guard against attacks from unexpected directions. In the same vein, Sun Tzu realized that attacking the enemy's strategy and foiling his plans before attacking his army would weaken him significantly, making the physical destruction of his forces easier. Ultimately, success requires intricate knowledge of the enemy and oneself.

The physical destruction of the enemy forces is but half of the aim of the offensively minded fighter. The other half entails moral destruction. He who loses his fighting spirit can no longer engage in battle with hope of victory. Herein lies the importance of helping the adversary lose the battle gracefully. A revealing example from history might be Germany's loss in World War I versus Japan's loss in World War II. The Versailles Treaty signed at the conclusion of World War I between Germany and the Allied Powers called for Germany to accept full responsibility for the war and pay enormous reparations, a demand which gravely humiliated the German people and prompted them to rise again. By contrast, the Japanese population was quicker to accept their unconditional surrender to the Allies at the conclusion of World War II. The promise that they could retain their emperor as a living symbol of Japan also helped them retain their pride as a people.

Like Sun Tzu, Carl von Clausewitz believed that combat should be a brief, concentrated effort in order to minimize losses. But, unlike Sun Tzu, he favored direct attack against the opposing force much like a boxer relying on a knockout to win the fight. He agreed that numerical superiority (physical strength) and the concentration of force against the critical point, or what he called "the hub of all power and movement," is crucial to the destruction of the enemy force.[4] "The best strategy," he said, "is *always to be very strong* [italics in the original], first generally then at the decisive point."[5] While numerical superiority comes in degrees and is not necessarily decisive, he acknowledged that a numerically inferior combatant emerging victorious against much greater odds constitutes the exception rather than the rule.

Furthermore, Clausewitz demonstrated little room for benevolence in his analysis of war. He did not consider winning without bloodshed a realistic option, as reinforced through his statement that "[t]he destruction of the enemy's army is the key to his defeat."[6] The successful combatant thus seizes the initiative and destroys the opposing force while time is on his side:

> Let us not hear of Generals who conquer without bloodshed. If a bloody slaughter is a horrible sight, then that is a ground for paying more respect to War, but not for making the sword we wear blunter and blunter by degrees from feelings of humanity, until someone steps in with one that is sharp and lops off the arm from our body.[7]

The conduct of warfare can be divided into a number of principles, with the destruction of the enemy's military capacity of principal importance. Although diplomatic means can help maintain peace, they cannot necessarily secure peace. This chapter discusses the benefits of numerical superiority, the strengths of the offensive weapons, and the need for speed and aggression aimed at undermining the enemy's physical prowess and fighting spirit.

Key Points: Destroying the Enemy Force

Sun Tzu	Carl von Clausewitz
Foil the enemy's plans to weaken him before destroying his forces.	Seize the initiative in order to destroy the opposing force.
Striving for a positional advantage allows one to use strength against weakness and end the fight quickly.	Combat should be a brief, concentrated effort, relying on simple and direct attack with overwhelming force.
Sufficient numerical superiority is crucial to the destruction of the enemy force.	The best way to destroy the enemy is by disarming him or attacking the decisive point.
Lasting peace is secured by allowing the enemy to surrender gracefully.	Destroying the enemy's spirit is a step toward victory.

Numerical superiority or physical strength in the martial arts is only one factor of importance when securing victory, albeit a significant one. Sun Tzu recognized its importance by suggesting that a numerical superiority of five to one is necessary in order to attack the enemy successfully.[8] But he also acknowledged the limitations of numerical superiority. "In war, numbers alone confer no advantage," he said. Instead, you must "estimate the enemy situation correctly and then concentrate your strength to overcome the enemy."[9] He further noted that troops who are sick or weary from hardship can be defeated even if numerically superior. Ideally, battle should be fought on your terms where you choose the time and place of the engagement, thereby increasing your relative strength advantage: "[H]e who occupies the field of battle first and awaits his enemy is at ease, and he who comes later to the scene and rushes into the fight is weary."[10]

Clausewitz agreed that superiority in numbers is crucial and, like Sun Tzu, advocated striking the enemy with a force that is significantly stronger. He further stressed the importance of combining numerical superiority with attack directed at the decisive point, because such a strategy can effectively "be a counterpoise to all the other cooperating circumstances."[11] For example, even the martial artist who is physically superior to his enemy might consider an attack directed against the eyes or ears, because an enemy who cannot see cannot fight, and an enemy who cannot maintain balance cannot fight. (The inner ears contain the sensory organs for balance, and to this effect they constitute the "hub of all movement.") On the other hand, a martial artist who lacks the physical strength to attack with overwhelming force, and who is not in position to attack a critical target, must decide whether or not he can defeat the opposition through other means such as deception or positioning. Consider two boxers circling each other in a ring. The tactically dominant boxer strives to retain the superior position by avoiding moves that might get him cornered or placed with his back to the ropes.

Furthermore, as discussed in chapter 5, combat is a struggle of will. In one of his works from 1805, Clausewitz stated that a chief rule of politics is never to be helpless, and the objective of imposing one's will on the enemy can most readily be achieved by disarming him.[12] He who is unable to use his weapons—be it guns, knives, arms, or legs—will experience a sudden loss of confidence. A martial artist engaged in single man combat can achieve this goal by dislocating a joint or destroying the ligaments in his adversary's shoulder, elbow, or knee. The physical destruction of the adversary's weapons renders him incapable of resisting and counterstriking. But if he cannot be defeated outright, an option is to destroy his forces one at a time until he loses the strength and will to continue.

While aiming for the destruction of the enemy forces, there is simultaneously a second element of combat that must not be for-

Brazilian Jiu-jitsu offers some good examples of how the skilled fighter can progressively work his way closer to victory, through intimate familiarity with the human
anatomy and a clear understanding of the enemy's capabilities. *(Image source: Brian A.
Goyak, Wikimedia Commons)*

gotten: the safety and preservation of one's own forces. Little is
gained if both belligerents perish in the fight. Self-preservation, as
a negative element of combat because the enemy cannot be con-
quered through defense alone, thus complements the positive action of attack.

In unarmed hand-to-hand combat, attacking the enemy with
full intent of destroying his forces without risking a broken bone
or damaged ligament in the process requires a gradual strengthening of your weapons. Many martial arts focus on conditioning the
hands, feet, elbows, shins, and skull by striking a variety of training apparatus. For example, you may start by striking a focus mitt
or bag bare fisted, and after a few weeks of training graduate to
striking harder targets such as a makiwara board (a padded striking board or post with a rough surface). As your hands and feet
become conditioned to the impact, you may progress further by
pounding your fists into pellets or sand, and finally by breaking

The ability to break wood, ice, or bricks enhances the martial artist's confidence in his abilities to throw a strong strike without incurring an injury. *(Image source: James B. Hoke, Wikimedia Commons)*

boards, bricks, or ice. Critics of breaking view this practice as nothing but showmanship, claiming that it has little martial arts value. But it behooves one to remember that the ability to break a board or brick without fear of damaging the hand or foot gives the martial artist confidence to strike an adversary with full force in a real fight and persevere.

Muay Thai, an aggressive martial art from Thailand that focuses on doing maximum damage to an opponent, exposes the combatants' bodies to tremendous physical abuse. Also referred to as the art of eight limbs, the Muay Thai fighter's use of hands, feet, elbows, and knees makes him an extremely dangerous weapon at medium and close combat range. Thought to have originated nearly two thousand years ago as a hand-to-hand combat art, and later employed to battle the Burmese, Thailand's traditional enemy, Muay Thai was used in conjunction with weapons such as the curved knife and bladed staff for the purpose of demolishing the adversary. For example, a Muay Thai fighter might throw a front kick to momentarily halt a weapon attack, and then seize the initiative by counterattacking with a knife or staff. Note the similarity in concept to Western medieval swordsmanship, where the knight would use a kick to keep his opponent at bay if the distance proved unsuitable for a strike with the longsword. Before becoming a modern sport, Muay Thai fighters would wrap their hands in hemp ropes or strips of cotton for the dual purpose of protecting their hands against injury while inflicting wounds on the adversary. Sometimes, fragments of glass would be glued to the ropes.

The Muay Thai fighter trains for speed, accuracy, and power. Speed allows him to seize the initiative; accuracy enables him to attack the weakest part of the opponent's anatomy with a strong weapon; and power ends the fight. The elbows and knees are particularly feared weapons because their small impact surfaces give them sharp, penetrating power. Elbows and knees prove effective at close range, where they have the capacity to neutralize the power of an adversary well-versed in long range strikes and kicks. While the elbow derives its power from the full rotation of the body and, aimed at the jaw or temple, can end the fight instantly, the power of the knee is increased by grabbing an opponent around the neck and pulling him forward and into the strike without rotating the body. Knees are used as preparatory weapons to wear the opponent down and open him to a knockout.

The Muay Thai kick thrown to the legs may be one of the most devastating weapons invented in unarmed combat. The relentless pounding of the opponent's outside thigh area is aimed at the physical destruction of his foundation and thus his ability to remain in the battle. To fully understand the value of this strategy, consider how all styles of martial arts focus on building a strong stance for the purpose of generating powerful strikes and kicks. A Muay Thai kick with the shin aimed at the opponent's foundation can generate enough force to break bones, drop the opponent to the ground, and cause the total destruction of his combat capability. If thrown to the body, a kick with the shin can easily break a rib and damage the internal organs, ending the fight instantly.

Siamese King Naresuan fighting the Burmese crown prince at the battle of Yuthahat-thi in 1593 CE. Muay Thai was developed from a hand-to-hand weapon art employed by the Thais against their traditional Burmese enemy. *(Image source: Heinrich Damm, Wikimedia Commons)*

A Muay Thai boxer who has strengthened his shins through repeated training can kick with full intent of doing damage without fear of injury, and without wearing protective equipment. This is important because fear of injury tends to have a negative psychological effect on the fighter and can cause him to relinquish the initiative. Furthermore, since Muay Thai was developed for the battlefield and not the ring, every move has to count. Defensive blocks are viewed as offensive strikes. The elbows, which are strong, hard, and pointed, make excellent blocking weapons. An elbow block aimed at the opponent's front or roundhouse kick ideally has enough power to shatter his shin bone. Since the traditional goal of the Muay Thai fighter is to destroy the enemy force, injuries in sports competition remain high. Muay Thai fighters who start training at a young age normally retire from competition by their mid-twenties.

Practitioners of the Japanese fighting styles may be particularly noteworthy for their ability to destroy the enemy force. Many Japanese martial arts encourage the practitioners to train bare fisted to harden their weapons and gain the confidence they need to take a strike as well as dish it out. Those training for combat rather than point sparring learn to throw several strikes and kicks in succession, relentlessly pounding the opponent into submission. Breaking boards, bricks, and ice, although inanimate objects, conditions the fighter to strike with penetrating power. Suppleness and flexibility are also crucial to injury avoidance. The fighter who is tense cannot respond to a threat as quickly as he who is supple, and can be controlled easier by the opponent. Flexibility further enables the martial artist to use his hands and feet interchangeably, for example, by kicking the opponent in the head from close range, thus increasing his destructive capability.

Practitioners of kyokushin karate, founded by master Masutatsu (Mas) Oyama (1923-1994 CE), train hard in full contact fighting, often without gloves and other protective equipment to achieve an unbreakable fighting spirit and a tough body that can endure severe punishment. Each attack is done with full intent of doing damage. Typical techniques include the fist impacting with the knuckles of the first two fingers, the hand sword impacting with the outer edge of the hand, the elbow and forearm, and the knife edge, ball, heel, and instep of the foot. Emphasis is placed on mental conditioning. Since the mind leads the body, he whose spirit is broken cannot command his body in battle and is thus technically destroyed. The skilled kyokushin practitioner can eliminate distracting thoughts of pain and death and focus only on achieving the victory.

Shotokan karate, founded by Gichin Funakoshi (1868-1957 CE) with roots in Okinawa, is a martial art that likewise excels in destructive capability. The deep stances of shotokan facilitate strength and power with emphasis on linear moves and economy of motion by taking the most direct route to the target. Typical techniques include reverse punches, front kicks, and sweeps, with kicks aimed primarily below the waist. The combat philosophy behind the art is "to kill with one blow."[13] Each technique is therefore developed for maximum penetrative power.

However, the Korean martial arts may prove particularly interesting to study for their spectacular techniques aimed at the destruction of the enemy force. In addition to employing hard throws that will immediately destroy the enemy's capacity to retaliate, hapkido is highly effective for destroying the adversary's weapons and combat efficiency. Through a combination of hard strikes, violent throws, and brutal joint locks, the hapkido practitioner does every move with full intent of ending the fight quickly. Should you find yourself on the receiving end of a hapkido joint lock, you will know beyond a shadow of a doubt that, in an environment away from the training hall where you are not afforded the luxury of tapping out, the tiniest technique progression will incapacitate you immediately.

Success in hapkido depends on accuracy in strikes, kicks, and joint manipulation techniques. A single blow directed at a vulnerable target, such as the opponent's upper chest or heart, has the capacity to drop him to the ground instantly. The mindset is that you may not get a second chance, so the first defensive move against the adversary's attack must be done with maximum force. A kick to

Taking the opponent off balance, for example, by catching his leg as he kicks, followed by a knee dislocation technique will destroy his foundation as well as his weapon (his leg). (*Image source: Nathan Hall, Wikimedia Commons*)

dislodge a weapon from his hand, for example, must be thrown with accuracy in order to have the intended effect. The hapkido practitioner must also have the technical expertise to proceed with a joint lock without delay. Techniques designed to flow with the opponent's momentum rely on quick and sharp reversals of direction. A forceful break of the adversary's wrist will result in immediate destruction of his combat capability. Catching the leg of a kicking opponent must likewise be done with speed and full intent of doing damage. A takedown followed by a dislocation of the knee joint would afford the adversary no opportunity to struggle against the technique.

Like hapkido, taekwondo is an extremely punishing martial art. Although Olympic style taekwondo is a modern invention, traditional taekwondo has ancient origins and was developed for combat to the death. Hand techniques are used on occasion, but practitioners rely primarily on a large arsenal of high and low kicks and can deliver blows with tremendous destructive power. Kicks can be thrown to any target but are primarily aimed at the adversary's head and neck. Speed is the key to power and minimizes target exposure particularly in spinning techniques. The thrust of the hip in combination with the rotation of the body generates a force that will drop the adversary and end the fight instantly. Keeping the arms and legs close to the body throughout the spin naturally facilitates speed and aids the martial artist with balance. Like the spin kick, the front kick is effective because of the momentum created by the large leg muscles. Front kicks are often used in combination where the first kick draws the desired reaction and the second kick ends the fight. For example, a front kick delivered to a low target such as the body or groin will stun the adversary and either force him to step back or lean forward. The next kick is then thrown to the head to knock him out. Although the full sequence of techniques that destroys the enemy's combat capability includes only two kicks thrown in rapid succession, an opponent will unlikely survive the attack intact.

The taekwondo axe kick, dropping from above the head straight down into the target with the aid of gravity, likewise relies on the large muscles in the leg for power and has the capacity to end the fight in a knockout, broken bones, or shock. An axe kick landing on the shoulder can incapacitate the opponent's arm by breaking the clavicle, resulting in the destruction of that weapon. Impacting the target with the heel of the foot further concentrates the force over a small surface area, resulting in maximum damage with minimum effort. As a dynamic art that relies on relentless attacks to defeat the enemy, those facing a skilled taekwondo practitioner in battle naturally need a great deal of courage.

As demonstrated through these examples, the physical destruction of the enemy proves common in martial arts of Asian origin. The Western "way of war" adheres to many similar philosophies. Clausewitz believed that the simple and direct attack with overwhelming force is superior to any attack involving extensive maneuvering or long sequences of techniques that can easily be foiled by the enemy. If, at any time during the execution of a complex maneuver, one is subjected to friction or chance, improvisation may not be possible. Thus, the initiative typically rests with the aggressive fighter who uses direct attack and simplicity over complexity. Economy of motion, Clausewitz informed us, is the key to success: "Our opinion is not on that account that the simple blow is the best, but that we must not lift the arm too far for the time given to strike."[14]

For example, as demonstrated in small circle jujitsu developed in Hawaii by Wally Jay, functionality with respect to smooth transitioning from one technique to another facilitates economy of motion in accordance with the principle of never lifting "the arm too far . . ." Most importantly, mastering technique transitions enables the practitioner to control the opponent and be prepared for unforeseen changes. Success depends on exerting continuous pain, communicating to the adversary that a break or joint dislocation is imminent.[15] Small circle jujitsu is primarily about controlling the opponent from a standing position; the goal is not to go to the ground with him. A relative strength advantage can be gained by attacking a weakness in his anatomy. For example, a strike can seldom be caught in midair successfully, but a block against an opponent's punch can open an opportunity for a joint lock technique, as can any grab against the upper body. If the opponent reaches out to push, the small circle jujitsu practitioner can take advantage of the motion by pivoting his upper body to the side, placing the opponent's hand within easy reach for a counter-technique. A quick trap of the adversary's hand will stabilize the motion, allowing the practitioner to proceed with a finger lock. The pain is instantaneous, giving the adversary no chance to counter the move. He has but one choice: to submit or risk incapacitation.

Several distinct Western combat arts also stress the destruction of the enemy force. Savate, developed in France in the early 1800s for use on the streets as a means of survival, relies primarily on kicks to stop an attacker; although, strikes when used often result in knockout. The savate fighter prefers kicks to strikes because street fights in early nineteenth century France had taught the fighters that the legs were capable of delivering blows far more devastating than punches. Since savate was practiced in abundance in Marseille, a port town in southern France, it is speculated that it drew its techniques from a mix of Asian fighting styles brought to France from sailors returning from Asia, coupled with Basque fighting styles as a

Savate, also known as French foot fighting, is a Western combat art with emphasis on kicking skills. Note the shoes that are typically worn in training and competition. (*Image source: Daniel, Wikimedia Commons*)

result of the Basque influence in southern France.[16] A distinguishing characteristic of savate is the use of reinforced shoes similar to wrestling shoes. (Savate means "old shoe" or "wooden shoe.")

Geared toward full contact fighting with focus on hard training and sparring, and kicks to keep the brawler at a distance, savate is unique among street fighting styles. The savate practitioner's emphasis on techniques considered essential in street fights, while ignoring forms practice and spirituality, makes him a tough opponent in a battle that has as its goal to incapacitate the enemy. Accuracy in strikes and kicks is naturally important. Savate proved particularly useful among sailors fighting onboard ships on a rolling sea, where ropes and other structures could be used to help the practitioner maintain balance when kicking. For example, a savate fighter delivering a spin kick to his adversary's head would use the deck of the ship for support, by dropping down with his hands almost as if doing a cartwheel. (Note the similarity in concept to the kicks of capoeira.)

As a combat art used by the French police and military elite, savate kicks are aimed at low, medium, or high targets, and are also used to compromise an adversary's balance. Although the savate fighter frequently throws kicks to the head because of the vulnerability of this target and the likelihood that it will end the fight, a kick to the knee of an advancing opponent will destroy his leg and thus his capacity to retaliate. The stop-kick, thrown like a front kick but with the toes turned outward from the centerline, proves particularly practical because it can be driven through the target with the fighter's full weight behind it, yet requires no rotation of the body. Economy of motion is therefore preserved. Impacting with the bottom of the foot rather than the ball, heel, or toes further minimizes the risk of missing the target. A stop-kick aimed at the thigh just above the knee, hyper-extending the adversary's leg, will stop his advance instantly.

Sweeps, a trademark of savate, are set up with aggressive punches, driving the opponent to the rear and compromising his balance. Since the sweep itself will not destroy the enemy force, it must be delivered to a sensitive target such as the Achilles tendon. Preferably, both legs should be swept simultaneously. An added advantage of the sweep is that an adversary who is taken to the ground repeatedly must expend a great deal of energy getting back to his feet and will eventually tire and become useless in combat. In the same vein, kicks thrown to the arms will not only injure the opponent, but tire him and render him incapable of continued offense. However, the spirit of the competitive savate fighter tells him to reject defeat. As long as his legs are intact, he can fight even if his arms are damaged.

To further emphasize the importance the savate practitioner places on kicking, punches in competition must be thrown in combination with kicks. For example, jabs can be used to set up the finishing kick by prompting the opponent to bring his hands up to defend against a strike aimed at his face. A quick follow-up roundhouse kick with the ball of the foot, or with the toes if wearing shoes, can easily break the opponent's ribs. The same kick aimed at an organ such as the liver or kidney can drop the opponent to the ground. Driving the knuckles of the hand into the adversary's face followed by a kick to his midsection or lower ribs with the tip of a hard shoe would likely render him incapable of continued fighting.[17]

If one is unable to completely overthrow the enemy or destroy his forces, what options remain? Although some martial artists believe that the benevolent fighter should only do the amount of damage needed to secure safety, Clausewitz recognized that in an activity as dangerous as war, the desire to appear benevolent can backfire, giving the enemy the power to rise again. He said, "[c]ombat is the only effective force in war; its aim is to destroy the enemy's forces as a means to a further end."[18] However, he acknowledged that a conflict does not have to be "mutual murder." Victory can also be achieved by "killing the enemy's spirit rather than his men."[19] Like Sun Tzu, he spoke of the importance of taking the enemy by surprise. The relative strength advantage gained through unorthodox fighting techniques can have the effect of breaking the opponent's morale and fighting spirit. In fact, killing his spirit may be a surer way to victory, because an enemy who acknowledges defeat has taken the first step toward constructing a lasting peace. This is an area where Asian and Western military theories converge. According to the Chinese military classic, *The Methods of the Ssu-Ma*, physical strength allows one to endure the hardships of battle, but spirit helps one secure the victory.[20] Allowing the enemy to surrender gracefully is of great importance, because without the option of surrender an enemy will be compelled to fight to the death, prolonging the battle and potentially increasing the losses for all involved.

To fully appreciate Sun Tzu and Clausewitz, however, one must guard against taking their statements out of context. While winning without bloodshed is ideal, as a participant in China's long and brutal war history, Sun Tzu understood that blood would likely be shed before the battle was over. Clausewitz, by contrast, while defining war as physical battle, acknowledged that some conflicts can be resolved through diplomatic means. Only if one wants to overthrow the enemy's military powers must there be a physical engagement ending in the destruction of his military capability. The participants in battle can also take an offensive or defensive stand depending on the objective: to destroy the enemy force or defend against such destruction; to take territory or defend territory. The offensive or defensive nature of the objective will determine how one approaches combat. For example, a martial artist may be fighting a purely defensive battle with the aim of driving the enemy away. The total destruction of his forces may not be necessary if an aggressive display of mental superiority will convince him to back down and leave the property.

However, in conflicts where combat does not actually take place, the idea of combat must still be at the heart of each belligerent. While delay, caution, and diplomacy can prove more valuable than dashing headfirst into battle, objectives cannot be met unless the martial artist also projects a physical and mental readiness to engage the enemy with the aim of destroying his forces and thus his combat capability.

CHAPTER 7

STRENGTH OF THE DEFENSIVE POSITION

"One defends when his strength is inadequate; he attacks when it is abundant." — **Sun Tzu**

"Defense is the stronger form of war." — **Carl von Clausewitz**

Military historian John Keegan argues that China has historically focused on defense and pacifist ways of war, such as caution, delay, and avoidance of battle over offense and face-to-face confrontation.[1] However, as explained in *The Seven Military Classics of Ancient China*, "Defense does not end with just the completion of the walls and the realization of solid formation. One must also preserve spirit and be prepared to await the enemy."[2] Defense works only in conjunction with offense for winning the political objective. It is relied upon when in the inferior position, because it allows the weaker fighter to preserve energy (thus, it is the stronger form of war). But defense does not imply passivity. Good defense has several aims: protect you from harm, destroy the enemy's ability to fight by tiring him, and create an opportunity for offense.

Sun Tzu's saying that "[t]hose skilled in defense conceal themselves in the lowest depths of the Earth," and "[t]hose skilled in attack move in the highest reaches of the Heavens,"[3] suggests that action is more heroic than non-action. Although defense without counterattack can fulfill the immediate aim of protecting one from harm, it is useless in the long run because it fails to destroy the opposing force. Like offense, and in order to serve the end goal of victory, defense must be executed with correct timing; it must interfere with the opponent's offense and provide an opportunity to seize the initiative. Deceptive practices are particularly appropriate for the weaker fighter, because it allows him to attack when the enemy does not expect it. As underscored in the principle of nonresistance, use strength when the opponent is weak and yield when he is strong.

Unlike Sun Tzu who promoted deception aimed at increasing the relative strength of his forces, Carl von Clausewitz favored offense over defense for reaching the political objective. He who takes the initiative, he argued, will act with increased morale and can concentrate his strength against the decisive point. However, he understood that conditions favoring the opponent cannot be overcome unless action is delayed and strength shifted to the weaker or less advantaged side. The hope is that the opponent will exhaust himself prematurely. "War," he pointed out, "begins with defense. The offensive does not lead to war unless the side which is attacked responds; this is why reciprocity is central to understanding war's nature. The big advantage enjoyed by the defender is time."[4] Defense has a negative aim: to avoid the aggressor's purpose. Offense, by contrast, has a positive aim; for example, to acquire treasure or force the enemy into submission. Without a reciprocal exchange of blows, however, there will be no conflict worthy of the name war, combat, or battle. It must thus be recognized that defense is not passive even though its immediate objective is. Delayed action merely prepares the defender for the counterattack. The changeover from defense to offense should happen as soon as the defender has determined that it will benefit him.

This chapter discusses the relationship between offense and defense and why defense is the stronger form of war. Although the martial artist can use defense successfully as a strategic measure to preserve or build strength, he cannot use it as a tactical measure with any degree of success. He must eventually convert defense to offense, because no battle is won through defense alone.[5] Blocks, evasion, positional superiority, and deterrence are defensive means by which offense is created with the aim of winning the objective.

Key Points: Strength of the Defensive Position

Sun Tzu	Carl von Clausewitz
Use strength when the opponent is weak, and yield when he is strong.	Defense should be abandoned when there is adequate strength to pursue the objective.
Wait until the enemy can be conquered, then attack him.	Time allows the weaker side to replenish its forces and counter with strong offense.
Protracted battle should be avoided, but suspension of action and the use of deception are strategic choices that lead to victory for the weaker fighter.	Action in war should only be suspended by the weaker side, and only if it will bring one favors.
He who is well prepared and lies in wait for an enemy who is not well prepared will be victorious.	He who understands the enemy can affect a sudden powerful transition from defense to offense when the enemy is the most vulnerable.

We can think of defense as sitting quietly behind a wall or barrier, holding up a shield or blocking an attack. But the goal of a defensive block or parry in the martial arts is to pave the way for the counterattack by stalling the opponent's momentum and creating an opportunity for retaliation when he is weak or unprepared. In Classical times, armies used shield walls when advancing toward the enemy on the battlefield. The shields protected against weapon attacks and allowed the bearers to force the enemy into retreat. Defense executed with correct timing thus interfered with the opponent's offense and caused "friction" that denied him the victory. In similar fashion, a Muay Thai boxer, for example, can defend against a knee strike and cause friction by placing his hands on the opponent's hips, preventing him from extending the hip even while his weapons remain technically intact.

In hand-to-hand combat, the fighter who has great defensive skills alongside of great endurance will likely defeat an opponent of great offensive skills but not as great endurance. Picture two boxers engaged in a bout. He who is stronger unleashes enormous offense from the start with the intent of destroying the opponent's physical capability to fight. But the physically weaker fighter with great defensive skills covers up and is thus able to absorb the blows by taking them on nonlethal targets such as the arms. Good defense naturally requires great composure when under attack. When the attacker wears out physically, the defender retaliates with a barrage of strikes. If his timing is sound, he has a good chance of winning the fight.

Defense is also about movement and evasion. The skilled boxer uses footwork to evade an attack; he ducks and slips punches (moves his head side-to-side); he controls the center of the ring, forcing the adversary to expend energy through excessive maneuvering. Evasive movement proves particularly important to the physically weaker fighter against an aggressive opponent who presses the attack. Controlling the center of the ring allows him to funnel the opponent into a corner, limiting his mobility and power. Defensive bobbing and weaving is also beneficial because it places the boxer in a superior position toward his adversary's side or back. The time is now ripe for counterstriking with a hook or straight strike to the head. Every time the offense-minded boxer unleashes a strike he will be punished, not by trading blow for blow, but by his opponent's superior use of defense.

But even an exceptionally skilled boxer cannot duck and slip his way through a three-minute round without throwing a single strike and expect to win. In war, a well-entrenched defense must counter-fire at the enemy and destroy him as he is closing the distance. A purely defensive boxer might win by default, for example, if the offensive boxer accidentally twists his ankle and cannot continue the match, but this would not be viewed as a true victory and a rematch would likely be scheduled at some future date. Furthermore, the purely defensive boxer would get disqualified, because there can be no match if he does not agree to physically engage his opponent. In war, the trench might allow a weaker army to preserve strength, but the counter-blow must eventually come in order to destroy the opposition.

It is thus clear that the boxer must capitalize on defense at an opportune moment. Good defense places him at close combat range and at a superior angle away from the opponent's line of power. Ideally, his counterstrike should come when the opponent is mentally imbalanced and needs time to regain his composure. Good defense allows the physically weaker boxer to preserve energy at a minimal cost while seizing the initiative for the counterattack. The important part to remember is that offense and defense are directed toward the same goal—victory—and attack is the "pivotal point of defense."[6]

The idea that one type of warfare (defense) contains elements of the other (offense) is apparent in Asian writings. *The Seven Military Classics of Ancient China* discusses the integration of various counterparts of warfare, such as *ch'i* (indirect) and *cheng* (direct). For example, "some [forces] use spies to be successful; others, relying on spies, are overturned and defeated."[7] The trick is knowing when to use indirect versus direct attack; when to rely on defense versus offense, or, in some cases, how to integrate defense and offense, for example, by jamming an elbow into the opponent's shin as defense against a roundhouse kick.

The shaolin kung-fu "splashing hands" system of fighting, so named because the movement of the hands mimic shaking off water, focuses on simultaneous defensive and offensive techniques geared toward street fighting, in addition to explosive high-speed movement such as quick shuffles to avoid the opponent's line of power while closing the gap, and straight kicks aimed at low targets. The number of strikes delivered in rapid succession combined with the shuffle promotes deception and makes this martial art ideal for stifling the opponent's offense. The splashing hands system relies on close range fighting coupled with checks and blocks, and the skilled practitioner seizes the initiative by making the first move, drawing a desired reaction from the adversary. When the opponent attempts to withdraw from the attack, the practitioner reverts to offense while remaining at close range, giving the adversary no opportunity to distance himself or regain his composure. Close range fighting and timing is refined through two-person drills performed in the training hall.[8]

Wing chun kung-fu likewise focuses on simultaneous defense and attack through its close range multiple strike philosophy. Deflections and evasive moves coupled with forward pressure double as offense, or at the very least pave the way for the skilled martial artist by allowing him to capitalize on a defensive move as soon as an opening appears in the adversary's guard. Kenpo karate is yet an interesting martial art to study because it provides several demonstrations of how offense exists within defense. For example, when the opponent grabs the kenpo practitioner's lapel, he steps back and outside of the opponent's reach for the punch or kick that must certainly follow, simultaneously pinning the opponent's hand to his lapel and striking upward against the elbow of his outstretched arm. The mere fact that the kenpo practitioner stepped back in defense, however, forced the opponent's arm to extend, which assisted the kenpo practitioner's offensive strike against the elbow. Defense was thus converted to offense. For further analysis of the interaction between defense and offense, consider how kata in most styles of karate begin with a defensive technique and, following the defense, immediately implements an offensive technique to demonstrate that defense by itself is not enough to win the fight. Many of the offensive techniques are maiming blows aimed at a vital target such as a joint or nerve center.

As demonstrated through these examples, combat is the continual interaction between opposing forces with an escalation in power resulting in one side emerging victorious. Since it includes elements of attack and defense and both belligerents strive to conquer, there is no true equilibrium between forces. Rather, defense is the immediate aim of the weaker fighter in order to ensure his survival. In other words, he who chooses to suspend action does so not as an act of cowardly submission, but with the knowledge that it will bring him favors. Consider in the grappling arts how a simple cover-up can help one preserve strength while waiting for an opportunity to counterattack. The guard position (on your back with the opponent between your legs) proves effective because of the limits it places on the opponent's movement and ability to attack. Options for a counterattack include an arm bar, a choke, and a variety of wrist and finger holds. For example, the defender can use his legs which are to the outside of the opponent's body to apply a triangle choke. Mixed martial arts have gained enormous popularity through the display of good strategy and tactics in offense and defense.

Brazilian Jiu-jitsu with its arsenal of chokes, wrist and arm locks, and leg and ankle locks may prove particularly interesting when studying the strength of the defensive position. An opportunity for a counterattack will be present the moment either fighter extends a limb toward the other. Since he who controls the other holds the initiative also in defense, the goal of the Brazilian Jiu-jitsu practitioner is to seize control and impose his will on the opponent, preventing him from executing his techniques as intended. For example, an opponent on his back or side can be controlled with an arm bar. By pushing his weight into an opponent on his knees, the Brazilian Jiu-jitsu fighter can control the movement of the adversary's hip and virtually immobilize him, thus gaining the option of moving to a stronger position for the counterattack. How successful he is has to do with his ability to recognize the opponent's weaknesses in each position he assumes, and taking action against them. Chokes, for example, can be applied from the front, rear, and side, in figure-four fashion, or as cross-collar chokes. Having intimate knowledge of the workings of the human body aids the Brazilian Jiu-jitsu fighter in the anticipation of the next move, and helps him lure the opponent into inadvertently placing himself in a position of defeat.

Relying on defense as the stronger form of war also means that one must exercise patience, waiting for the enemy to make a mistake that can be exploited. Brazilian Jiu-jitsu is ideal for turning the opponent's power against him through its many leverage concepts. The supine position, which is considered weak in most martial arts, can be an advantage in Brazilian Jiu-jitsu. When an opportunity to

Wrestlers are known for their knowledge of how to manipulate the balance of an opponent from the defensive position, as demonstrated in the techniques used by these ancient pankrationists. Note the lock around the ankle. (*Image source: Matthias Kabel, Wikimedia Commons*)

convert to offense arises, for example, when a straddling opponent makes a mistake that momentarily jeopardizes his balance, the skilled Brazilian Jiu-jitsu fighter can topple him, grab an extended limb, and execute a lock against the elbow, shoulder, or ankle.

As summarized in these examples, although defense is typically assumed by the weaker or physically inferior fighter, it is the stronger form of war because it allows him to preserve energy and counterattack at a time of his choosing. The martial arts require courage and the summoning of one's total physical capacity. As further demonstrated in the Ultimate Fighting Championship, combat does not consist of a single decisive blow, but of a succession of blows where the weapons—arms, legs, body, and mind—are coordinated for maximum power and effect. The first strike merely creates a favorable condition for each successive strike. (The mind is not a weapon per se but refers to a rational element comprised of good judgment. A fighter with a clear mind can see "through the confusion of [battle] to its core and then [take] decisive action."[9])

Both Sun Tzu and Clausewitz stressed the importance of defeating the opponent quickly in order to reach the political objective without incurring excessive losses. Although Communist leader and political theorist Mao Tse-tung (1893-1976 CE) favored protracted war, the Chinese army has historically valued speed over duration.[10] No action should be suspended in war. However, as observed in the early days of the Ultimate Fighting Championship when matches did not have time limits, deception and the defensive position were used by the physically inferior fighter as strategic choices leading to victory with some matches lasting in excess of thirty minutes. The grappling arts, pioneered by the Gracie clan in the 1990s, demonstrate how a protracted battle can bring victory over a physically stronger opponent if your endurance and patience are strong enough. Eventually, you must fire back, however, or the opposing force will remain intact, break through your defenses, and emerge victorious.

Moreover, while the attacker typically holds the advantage of the initiative in any battle, the defender holds the advantage of surprise. Once the defender decides to counterattack, the attacker will be forced to go on the defensive, particularly if he is tired after having thrown a barrage of blows. The fight has now turned in favor of the defender. Thus, before choosing to fight a protracted battle, you must decide whether it is better waiting to launch your counterattack or taking advantage of the moment. If waiting turns the battle in favor of your opponent, it is better to take advantage of the moment and launch a forceful attack. However, if waiting allows you to preserve strength and emerge the superior fighter, this may be the better strategy.

Even martial artists who emphasize defense when entering a confrontation generally acknowledge the value of offense once it has been determined that their strength is adequate. Defense is also used to gain an edge after enticing the attacker to make the first move. How do you create this advantage? One way is by using the blocking weapon as a weapon of offense, for example, by striking a pressure point simultaneous to blocking the opponent's strike. Another way is by redirecting the strike through the use of minimal force, disrupting the opponent's timing and power and providing openings for the counterattack. Rather than giving up the initiative, you take it through defensive action by creating a favorable opportunity that brings you closer to victory.[11]

Hapkido practitioners typically demonstrate how to neutralize a threat through defensive action while causing "disorientation with minimal effort followed by a disabling attack."[12] The encounter

It has been said that offense is the best defense. Many martial arts and systems of self-defense focus on striking a vital point simultaneous with the defensive move. For example, an elbow strike to the sternum of an aggressive opponent can effectively aid an unbalancing technique. (*Image source: Ken Melton, Wikimedia Commons*)

starts with defense but ends with offense. The hapkido practitioner wins by exploiting the opponent's strength and counterstriking to a vital point. Although he who is strong in offense can take advantage of the defender by pressing the attack, he will likely expose a weakness sometime during the encounter. Consider also a sparring match where one of the participants relies on short bursts of strikes or kicks to overwhelm his opponent before falling back on footwork and movement to replenish his forces. The best time to start a counterattack is the moment the adversary reverts to defense, but before he has regained his composure and strength.

Aikido, by contrast, was developed based on the premise that it is a strictly defensive art, using neither strikes nor kicks to counter an opponent's attack. How does aikido function in relation to the idea that offense is the best defense and that one cannot win a fight through passive defense alone? The skilled aikido practitioner uses the attacker's momentum, evading the attack through superior timing rather than blocking it, and executing dynamic throws that will ideally send the adversary flying several feet away. Properly performed, aikido allows one to preserve energy against a stronger opponent while forcing him to expend energy. By adapting to the aggressor's offense, the aikido practitioner neutralizes the attack, often without inflicting permanent damage on the adversary. Like other defensive martial arts, aikido has a negative aim: to avoid the aggressor's purpose. But unlike many other defensive arts, it has no positive aim of destroying the enemy forces. The hope is that the aggressor will realize the folly of his ways and pursue a path to peace instead.

Aikido further advocates evasive moves for the purpose of decreasing the risk of sustaining an injury. This is particularly important if the enemy is wielding a weapon. The greater the force is behind the opponent's attack, the greater the momentum of the aikido practitioner's evasive move. For example, the motion of a front kick can be redirected with a sweeping vertical downward parry of the hand. The attack line is changed and energy preserved. As the opponent's momentum carries him forward, he becomes ripe for an unbalancing move. For example, the aikido practitioner might place his forearm across the opponent's upper body, directing him to the ground through a rearward sweeping spiral. The opponent will be perplexed that his kick missed the target and will attempt to kick again. But by then he has lost the initiative. As long as the aikido practitioner occupies the center of the circle, he can control the opponent's motion by going with it or reversing its direction. Reversing direction when controlling the center takes relatively little energy, which is why the move is so devastating to an opponent who occupies the outer edge of the circle. By continuing the motion or reversing its direction, the defender will constantly be evading the opponent's attempts to renew the attack. He will thus gain the initiative and ability to control the action without ever launching an offensive technique.

The aikido practitioner can likewise defend against a punch thrown to the head by controlling the attack line, redirecting the strike with a parry upward along his centerline while allowing the momentum of the strike to continue. He would now be in position to retaliate with offense; for example, with a knife hand strike to the opponent's neck. Or he might choose the gentler way and capitalize on the opponent's momentum by placing his forearm against the opponent's neck, controlling the center of the circle, and ending the fight with a throw that sends the adversary several feet away. Either way, the first defensive principle of aikido is avoidance of the attack and controlling the enemy by using correct and precisely timed techniques rather than pitting strength against strength.

However, a problem with a purely defensive art is that the opponent will likely refuse to accept defeat at the first parry or evasive move. A skilled aikido practitioner stays mentally ahead of his adversary, relying on *mushin*, or absence of thought as discussed in chapter 1. Absence of thought entails total awareness of the situation and is achieved through extensive experience in one's martial art. When the aikido practitioner achieves this state of mind after much practice, he can accept each attack as it comes toward him and with small and fluid movements capitalize on the opponent's momentum. The skilled aikido practitioner does not allow his energy to clash with the opponent; he does not violate the yin and yang by creating the condition for double-weightedness (exerting yang forces simultaneously with the opponent). Instead, when the opponent absorbs the momentum of his own attack, his focus will split with his main concern retaining balance. His own aggression will thus act as the agent of his defeat. Controlling the attack line and the center of the circle also allows the aikido practitioner to guide the offensive limb into a joint control technique with a number of options at his disposal: take the adversary to the ground, damage the joint, or force him to submit through pain compliance.

Aikido is a strictly defensive martial art that relies on controlling the center of the action, using the opponent's energy against him often through a weakness in his anatomy such as the wrist. Once the attack has been neutralized, the aikido practitioner can force the adversary to submit through pain compliance without actually damaging the joint. *(Image source: Magyar Balazs, Wikimedia Commons)*

A person engaged in a modern street encounter away from the training hall might use a defensive technique to momentarily stall the adversary's advance. His next step might be to launch a counterattack that will eliminate the threat. For example, he might start by bringing his arms up in front of his face to block a strike. The moment he blocks or avoids the blow, he reverts to offense by kicking the adversary's groin or elbowing him in the face. Failing to revert to offense will give the opponent the initiative, enabling him to break through the defensive barrier. Again, good defense must contain an element of offense. Preferably, the initial defensive technique should be instinctive, giving you momentary safety even in ambush. When you have gained a better sense of the nature of the threat, you can proceed with offensive action.

Battle can also be fought defensively in strategic terms, but offensively in tactical terms. This relationship between offense and defense can be observed in a self-defense situation; for example, a burglary of your home in the middle of the night. The burglar breaking into your home is invading your territory and is therefore on the strategic offensive. By contrast, you, the homeowner, are on the strategic defensive because you did not initiate the conflict. However, the moment you reach for the gun in the dresser drawer, the knife in the kitchen, or the phone in the office for the purpose of calling for help, you are on the *tactical* offensive. It is not absolutely necessary to aim for the total destruction of the enemy in every fight. Although the negative element of delayed action is not immediately as effective as the positive element of action, it might have a good success rate over time. When the opponent's energy expenditure is far greater than he expected, you may find a way to beat him physically or get him to agree to a peaceful settlement of your differences. The enemy might also choose to give up when he finds that far more effort is required to remain in the fight than what he had anticipated. But, by the same token, passive resistance will not destroy the enemy forces. The risk therefore exists that the enemy will attack you again at some future date.

How far can you take Clausewitz's tenet that defense is the stronger form or war? Since wars should be won as quickly as possible, action should not be suspended. However, if the enemy refuses to engage in the hope of finding a more favorable time for attack, the war *will* be suspended. But it can only be suspended by one side. Both sides would not agree to suspension, because then it would be peace and not war. If one side chooses to suspend the action, it does so in order to seek favors. The other side must then act without delay. By contrast, stalemates occur not because both sides agree to suspend the action but because the forces are evenly matched, or because the weaker force relies on defense as the stronger form of war and prolongs the battle. Thus, true equilibrium between the forces is never a part of warfare. Rather, both sides strive to conquer, and action will continue toward the climax until one side emerges victorious. Since war is divided into attack and defense, if you chose to suspend the action, your opponent would naturally prefer that you attack, and vice versa.

For further analysis, consider how you would classify a demonstration of power without actually exchanging blows? Is it defense

The physical display of power is evident in this ancient Roman mosaic picturing two boxers. Although a display of power can be a deterrent to battle, it must be supported by physical capability in order to serve a defensive purpose. Moreover, in a martial arts contest it is assumed that the fighters want to engage each other in physical battle. *(Image source: AlMare, Wikimedia Commons)*

or offense? Is it the stronger form of war? If you display a weapon or demonstrate your martial arts skills to a group of people, your reputation alone might communicate that you are a dangerous person, thus decreasing the risk that you will be attacked. You have now taken a defensive position through a display of offense. But, according to Clausewitz, this is not war, because war is about physical action and not deterrence.[13] Clausewitz further proposed that one should assume the defensive position only when one does not have the ability to seize the initiative. Defense is the stronger form of war only because it allows the weaker force to conserve strength while waiting for a good time to launch a counterattack. If you display your strength in front of others, you must also be physically and mentally ready to use it if push comes to shove. Morals aside, the person with superior strength should seek the initiative rather than focus on defense.

As discussed previously, and in contrast to Clausewitz, Sun Tzu advocated winning without engaging in combat. But how is this achieved? Should one publicly display one's forces as deterrence to battle, engage in diplomacy, or turn the other cheek? How would you classify a preemptive attack? Is it offense or defense? Is it the stronger form of war? Can you justify it morally through the perception of threat alone? Sun Tzu agreed that, although a public display of force may be used as a deterrent to conflict, the option to engage in combat must remain open in order for it to classify as combat or martial arts. The fact that your opponent knows that you have studied the martial arts but does not know how skilled you are can deter a fight altogether, or it can buy you time that allows you to preserve your forces until you can retake the initiative. Sun Tzu also emphasized deception as a defensive measure that would allow you to seize the initiative: Appear weak when you are strong and strong when you are weak.

As demonstrated through the examples in this chapter, although defense is the stronger form of war when fighting from a physically inferior position because it is generally "easier to hold ground than to take it,"[14] it is impossible to rely on defense alone. Doing so would mean that only one side is relying on offense, and there can be no war unless both sides exchange blows. In short, defense must have purpose; defense must be offensive, for example, through surprise or superior positioning. From a psychological perspective, offense is often the stronger form of war. Troops are generally more motivated to fight when they feel they are actively doing something. It is also true that the advantage generally lies with the attacker or the side who takes the initiative. But, while the offensive position ensures victory, as described in *T'ai Kung's Six Secret Teachings*, a defensive posture that is solid can accomplish its intended purpose and help the defender win the political objective over time. Once the decision is made to fight, one must be victorious, and offense and defense must play mutually interactive roles.[15]

Furthermore, the genius of military leadership lies in a combination of instinct and experience, or the ability to realize when defense has outlived its useful life. When you are pressed on your right, when your center is giving way, when you are overcome by the enemy forces, when it is impossible to move . . . it is either attack now or die. He who chooses to delay the fight by assuming the defensive position does so because his physical capacity is inferior to the enemy and not because he treasures a long war.

CHAPTER 8

FAILURE

"Know your enemy and know yourself, and in a hundred battles you will never be in peril."   — **Sun Tzu**

"The knowledge in war is very simple, but not, at the same time, very easy."   — **Carl von Clausewitz**

Sun Tzu recognized several human characteristics that prove detrimental to the soldier on the field of battle. A reckless fighter, for example, will be at greater risk of injury and death than a thoughtful fighter. Simultaneously, while he who is too impulsive can be provoked to commit an act that he will come to regret or that will jeopardize his safety, he who is overly afraid of death will be too cautious to prove effective; he will hesitate and forego the chance to score a victory. He further strove for maximum gain with minimum risk. As explored previously, conflicts should be ended quickly by making decisions based on knowing the enemy and yourself, and by using deception to turn the enemy's strength against him.

Carl von Clausewitz, by contrast, viewed boldness superior to timidity. His ideal way of war emphasized strength at the decisive point and the destruction of the enemy forces even at the risk of loss. Which approach is better? Although boldness will trump timidity which "implies a loss of equilibrium," a calculated caution should be part of the strategic plan.[1] A commander's intellect can lead an army in the proper direction and minimize downfalls. Failure, however, is a great teacher. As will be discussed in more detail in chapter 10, understanding that winning matters also in friendly competition will prompt one to study failure.

Analyzing how a technique can go wrong will bring insights into success and failure and empower you to make practical adjustments to your training regimen. Conducting a detailed study of failure will teach you about the steps required to avoid failure while broadening your understanding of techniques that work well or less well under a range of circumstances. Studying failure further opens the door to knowing your enemy and yourself, which Sun Tzu regarded as the cornerstone of success. Although success cannot be guaranteed no matter how well-planned your strategy, Clausewitz's *On War* likewise demonstrates that when the causes of failure are properly studied, the enlightened scholar can take action and decrease the risk of falling victim to chance.

The question that must be asked is what you are truly capable of achieving at any particular stage of the fight. Henry Ford (1863-1947 CE), American industrialist and founder of the Ford Motor Company, said that failure is the opportunity to begin again, more intelligently. Although a particularly disastrous failure might not afford one the opportunity to begin again, in general, failure, as miserable as it is, is a sobering experience that provides insights into one's strengths and weaknesses, prompting one to become a better and more intelligent martial artist. This chapter explores the common causes of failure with an eye toward knowing the enemy and yourself by identifying the essential elements of the different fighting styles.

Key Points: Failure

Sun Tzu	Carl von Clausewitz
Factors that commonly cause failure include lack of resources, lack of preparation, lack of discipline, failure to know the enemy, oneself, or the objective, disorganization, and lack of competence.	Factors that commonly cause failure include human weakness, lack of boldness, and friction or chance.

When two fighters of equal strength meet in battle, he with the greater command of strategic skill will generally prevail.	Boldness trumps timidity, but a calculated caution should be part of the strategic plan.
If you cannot choose your fights, you must revert to a strategy that increases your strength by dividing the opposing force.	Both sides will suffer losses in combat, but loss of moral forces is the chief cause of the decision.
Decrease the risk of failure by seizing the initiative through a preemptive attack.	Minimize friction by resorting to straight and direct moves rather than complex maneuvers.

Many martial arts techniques work well in the training hall because your practice partner has been conditioned to attack and stage a reaction to an attack in a premeditated way. For example, consider how an aikido practitioner might fare if the attack hap-

Experimenting with techniques designed to end a fight, under the guidance of a qualified instructor, will teach the practitioner what it takes to defeat an uncooperative opponent. (*Image source: Kaylee LaRocque, Wikimedia Commons*)

pens quicker than anticipated and he is unprepared to sidestep the strike and flow with the motion. Would an attacker who had never practiced aikido really be sent flying as far away and as smoothly as is often observed in the training hall? Studying failure will teach you why proper timing of your defense to the opponent's attack is crucial. In the same vein, although Sun Tzu underscored the importance of choosing your ground wisely, this is not always possible. A martial artist who is sitting down when suddenly attacked may be physically unable to sidestep the strike and flow with the motion. Whether or not you score the victory thus depends on a number of uncontrolled circumstances, including individual skill and the ability of the enemy to utilize the environment to his advantage.

Friction, as Clausewitz called it, becomes particularly evident when a martial artist of one style meets a martial artist of another style in battle. For example, a tactic popular with the wing chun kung-fu practitioner involves fighting from close range with the aim of tying up the adversary's arms or splitting his focus with a barrage of short range strikes. If the opponent is a skilled boxer whose strength rests with the use of his hands, an attack against the hands (the boxer's center of gravity) may be the determining factor that ends the fight. But the opposite outcome is also possible. A boxer with a considerable physical strength and reach advantage might throw a knockout punch before the wing chun practitioner has a chance to position inside of the boxer's range of power and use the tactical moves called for by his martial art.

The particular techniques used to defeat the adversary further differ between martial arts. Some arts focus exceedingly on stand-up fighting, others on grappling. Some arts are predominantly striking arts, others kicking arts. Some arts are hard styles relying on direct attack and quick knockout, others are soft styles relying on flowing motion and extensive maneuvering. Sun Tzu stated that victory comes to those who know when they can or cannot fight: "If I know our troops can attack, but do not know the enemy cannot be attacked, it is only halfway to victory. If I know the enemy can be attacked, but do not realize our troops cannot attack, it is only halfway to victory."[2] Knowing yourself means that you clearly understand your physical and mental limitations. If you are under-trained in certain aspects of the fighting arts, you should avoid fighting from that perspective. For example, a great karate fighter who has never trained in a grappling art would be wise to know his limitations and strive to end the fight before it goes to the ground. Knowing your enemy means that you clearly understand his strengths and weaknesses. Fighting a superb high kicker should be avoided at distances that allow him to capitalize on his kicks. Moving to close range and sweeping his supporting foot might be an option that eliminates his kicking ability. But this tactic represents the ideal way of war and is not necessarily an accurate representation of how the battle will ultimately go down.

No matter how extensive your training has been, it is highly im-probable that you will be skilled in all styles of martial arts. If your focus is stand-up fighting, superior grappling skills may take years to acquire. However, basic techniques relevant to combat, such as the benefits of a stable stance and ability to utilize movement to your advantage, may take only a few months to acquire and would increase your chances of surviving a ground fight as long as you also possess the mental qualities that make up a good fighter: endur-ance, perseverance, courage, and a desire to seize the initiative and win. Crucial to success is the understanding that an opponent who has as his goal to take you down must first close the distance regard-less of which specific technique he uses for the takedown (throw, sweep, joint lock, etc.) Ideally, you might use footwork to set up a long range kick from an unexpected angle. A skilled taekwondo practitioner, for example, would use his kicking strengths and time a well-placed kick to his adversary's head, knocking him out the moment he attempts to close the distance for a takedown.

Defense, as we have learned, is the stronger form of war, and an opponent who uses defense skillfully can interfere with your combat plan, making your attack fail even if you are the physically stronger fighter. How do you counter good defense? When your attempt to pound the opponent into submission on the ground fails, you must have the physical skill and mental composure to adapt, for example, by recognizing an opportunity to apply a joint control hold. But,

When pounding an opponent into submission fails, a skilled grappler can detect opportunities for adaptation and offset the effects of friction by making a move against a weak part of the anatomy, as demonstrated by this soldier defeating his opponent with an arm bar. *(Image source: Lynn Murillo, Wikimedia Commons)*

as Clausewitz stated, although the knowledge is very simple, it is at the same time not very easy. Knowing what needs to be done will not help you win the war, unless you also possess the relevant skills. What should be recognized from Sun Tzu's and Clausewitz's writings is that the discourse of combat, how we talk about it, is the ideal way of war but not how battle ultimately unfolds. We can take all of Sun Tzu's and Clausewitz's advice to heart and still fail. We may also well understand their analyses, yet be unable to apply the insights because we are not in position to choose the time and place of battle.

Sun Tzu and Clausewitz taught us that the nature of combat or the underlying principles remain constant. It matters little who you are, what part of the world you are from, or what styles of martial arts you have studied because human nature does not change. We can only work within the range of human anatomy and human emotions. For example, taking an adversary to the ground requires that you can manipulate his balance. Whether you do so by sweeping his leg, grabbing and throwing him to the ground, or us-ing a lock against his wrist or neck depends on which art you have studied. But the underlying principle of destroying his foundation remains constant. Friction and the uncertainty of battle likewise ap-ply to both belligerents regardless of which style you have studied. Human emotions such as anger or fear of failure will likewise strike all participants of battle. The best you can do is to minimize losses by educating yourself about the physical and mental state of your opponent and yourself, and by practicing your martial art with the intent of analyzing the common causes of failure.

Weapon practice may prove exceptionally valuable in this regard because it teaches the martial artist that defeat resulting in the to-tal destruction of his forces can be final. While an empty hand strike to a nonlethal target such as the arm can be forgiving, this is not necessarily true with a weapon strike. A blow with a staff or cut with a knife can prove permanently disabling no matter where it lands. Weapons also tend to neutralize the strength advantage of an empty-handed fighter. Training with weapons, even if one does not intend to carry a weapon, is invaluable for understanding the im-portance of precision and timing. The great Japanese swordsman Miyamoto Musashi reminded us that, "[w]hen one understands the use of weapons, he can use any weapon in accordance with the time and circumstances."[3]

Kobudo (ancient way to stop war), an Okinawan martial art em-ploying the staff as one of several weapons (staff, sai, tonfa, kama, and nunchaku), was used to fight the samurai in the invasion of the islands in 1609 CE. Practicing with a weapon, which is essentially an extension of the martial artist's arm, aids the development of preci-sion in unarmed combat and therefore helps minimize failure under stress when fine motor skills tend to deteriorate. Furthermore, kata or forms are frequently practiced in the martial arts as a way to en-hance confidence through muscle memory. A major benefit derived from kata practice is the control of rhythm, or the ability to exercise power at the appropriate time. Confusing the opponent and creat-ing a sense of unpredictability by breaking his rhythm aids the mar-tial artist who must fight from a position of numerical inferiority.

Weapons are invaluable for teaching respect for combat and reminding the practitioner that a single blow can prove fatal. *(Image source: Blmurch, Wikimedia Commons)*

Kobudo forms with the staff employ many power moves in combination with strikes (pokes) to specific targets. Each strike and move is emphasized to instill skill and precision in offense, defense, and movement, thus minimizing the risk of failing to defend and counter another weapon-wielding fighter. Kobudo forms differ from the flashy musical kata that have become popular in competition and modern weapon demonstrations. The stress is not on showmanship but on practicality, always by understanding the dangers of facing an adversary wielding a weapon. Sun Tzu's principle of ending the fight quickly applies, as does Clausewitz's principle of minimizing friction by resorting to straight and direct moves rather than complex maneuvers.

We have now discussed a few options for surviving a fight against an opponent who is skilled in a martial art different from the one you have studied. But what can you do when fighting an opponent who is skilled in the same art as yours and the battle goes sour? Sun Tzu wrote the *Art of War* based on China's history of fighting an enemy of similar cultural biases, and could therefore outline precise principles of fighting. He underscored that when two fighters of equal strength meet in battle, he with the greater command of strategic skill (cunning, surprise, attacking the enemy's plans before attacking his army) will generally prevail. For example, a Muay Thai boxer facing another Muay Thai boxer in the ring knows in advance that he will encounter specific techniques such as elbows and knees, leg kicks, and takedowns, but will not encounter grappling techniques in a ground battle. He must therefore rely on strategic skill to beat his opponent. A Muay Thai fighter who fails in the ring does so primarily because he is weaker or less experienced than his opponent, or because he enters the fight low on confidence. A Brazilian Jiu-jitsu fighter facing another Brazilian Jiu-jitsu fighter likewise knows that he will encounter many techniques specific to grappling.

However, when the Ultimate Fighting Championship was instituted it was with the intent of pitting one style of martial art against another to "test" which style was superior when fighters were forced out of their comfort zones. When a Muay Thai champion meets a

Brazilian Jiu-jitsu champion in the ring, assuming that neither fighter possesses any noteworthy skills in the art of the other, an element
of unpredictability is brought to the action. Furthermore, away from
the competition arena, the reality of war is that we cannot precisely
know the fighting skills of our opponent. Although we can take
measures that will decrease the risk of failure by understanding
ourselves and our enemy, we cannot completely eliminate the element of friction. However, depending on the society in which you
live, certain techniques can be expected and the basic use of fists
and feet differs not much from one fighting style to another. Even
street brawlers with no martial arts training become predictable to
some extent, because human nature mandates the use of our fists
to pound an opponent into submission.

Other reasons why one may fail in combat include a lack of training or poor judgment. Although Sun Tzu rated numerical superiority highly, he recognized that in the reality of combat you may
not have the option of choosing your fights and must revert to a
strategy that increases your strength by weakening your opponent's,
for example, by dividing his forces. Many traditional Asian martial arts, as well as Brazilian Jiu-jitsu, excel at this concept, which
is why smaller or physically weaker fighters can defeat bigger or
stronger opponents. Adaptability is the key along with repetitious
training for the development of muscle memory. Although specific
techniques and defenses may lead to failure when a sudden change
occurs within the attack, constant repetition of techniques with
a partner brings confidence and ability to recognize and preempt
an imminent attack that you may otherwise have overlooked. As
a guide to the principles of combat, Sun Tzu's *Art of War* recommends seizing the initiative to offset the damaging effects of friction, for example, through a preemptive attack from an unexpected
angle that further allows you to retain full focus and control of the
fight. *Yizhan*, the idea of fighting a just war under the guise of a defensive posture, further warrants the use of a preemptive attack.[4]

As explored in chapter 3, practicing specific defenses to specific
attacks further helps the martial artist eliminate excessive thought
that leads to dangerous pauses in the middle of the action. As re-

inforced by the pragmatist Miyamoto Musashi, success comes by defeating the enemy at the start of the action, "so that he cannot rise again to the attack."[5] Every cut, even the way you grip a weapon, must be decisive and done with a resolute spirit.[6] The greater your ability to eliminate excessive thought, the greater your focus: "Whatever attitude you are in, do not be conscious of making the attitude; think only of cutting."[7]

Although the implementation of Sun Tzu's and Clausewitz's advice leads to risk reduction and increases the chance of scoring a victory, it does not guarantee victory. How well one does in battle has to do to some extent with the enemy's skill and fighting style. The combat capabilities of the opponent are difficult to measure

Fighter surprising his opponent by aggressively pressing the attack. Using the same style martial art as your opponent does not guarantee knowledge of his tactics or strategy, nor does knowledge guarantee successful action. Neither fighter enjoys monopoly on surprise. (*Image source: Indrek Galatin, Wikimedia Commons*)

and will fall outside of your control until you have taken some action to incapacitate him, which is why Sun Tzu placed particular weight on knowing the enemy before engaging him in battle. It naturally follows that unpredictability, such as broken rhythm, is of great value in the art of war. Unpredictability in technique can also give you a strength advantage by splitting the opponent's focus and dividing his forces. However, a weakness of Sun Tzu's teachings is that they fail to mention that neither side holds monopoly on surprise and deception.

Although the martial arts are numerous and encompass many variations, a good fighting art relies on some basic principles that, once learned, enable the practitioner to execute techniques also when the stress level is high and therefore reduce the risk of failure. Krav maga, for example, excels at eliminating unnecessary thought and keeping techniques simple yet effective. But even in arts that stress the use of complex moves, the reliance on principles rather than specific techniques helps one reduce the risk of failure, for example, by pressing the attack, disturbing the adversary's balance, attacking weak targets in his anatomy, using deception and surprise, attacking from unexpected angles, and preserving energy through good defense.

Furthermore, the adversary may attack armed or unarmed. He may use several tactics to defeat you, for example, a strike or kick, a grab or hold, or a throw through the use of flow or superior strength. A defensive technique against an armed attacker might fail because he has an absolute strength advantage through his weapon. Drawing the attack through a sudden unexpected move (except when a gun is involved) might give you the initiative and increase your defensive capabilities. Martial arts that focus on driving the opponent to the rear, such as wing chun kung-fu, effectively eliminate the opponent's ability to use strikes, kicks, and weapons by jeopardizing his foundation through aggressive movement. The practitioner of the fong ngan style of Chinese kung-fu likewise relies on aggressive advances inside of the opponent's range of power to jeopardize his balance and minimize the risk of failure, by delivering low kicks to the groin or leg hooks and sweeps followed by a strike intended to end the fight.[8]

According to Sun Tzu, the factors that commonly cause failure include lack of resources, lack of preparation, lack of discipline, failure to know the enemy, oneself, or the objective, disorganization, and lack of competence. Clausewitz listed human weakness, lack of boldness, and friction or chance. Specializing in training maneuvers particular to your martial art helps you seize the initiative and reduce the time it takes to react to a perceived threat. Although you cannot always know the enemy, knowing yourself is a starting point that gives you clear insight into your capabilities. Furthermore, by understanding the specific ways in which an opponent may attack you, you have taken a step toward Sun Tzu's dictum of knowing your opponent. Start by considering the essence of the particular martial art you are studying:

The Essence of Different Martial Styles

Aikido	Strictly defensive Japanese martial art that emphasizes control of a stronger opponent through the use of throws and joint locks over strikes and kicks. Practitioners of aikido neutralize aggressive action, using an opponent's force against him by bringing him into their circle of power. To successfully avoid and defend against or redirect an attack, the aikido practitioner must start his defense at the first indication of the attack.
Bartitsu	Hybrid gentlemanly martial art developed in England and precursor to the mixed martial arts. Incorporating a variety of combat ranges, practitioners of bartitsu draw strength from the techniques of boxing, judo, and jujutsu, fighting to the finish until the opponent can no longer use his weapons in offense or defense.

Brazilian Jiu-jitsu	Grappling and ground fighting art derived from Japanse jujutsu, requiring ability to recognize vulnerable positions and submitting the opponent through a choke or joint lock. In order to learn how to discern options for taking advantage of positional challenges, the Brazilian Jiu-jitsu practitioner must practice joint locks extensively to gain intricate knowledge of human anatomy.
Capoeira	Highly evasive Afro-Brazilian martial art stressing acrobatic maneuvers designed to deceive the enemy. Sweeps to the opponent's foundation and kicks to his head are common attacks. A skilled capoeira practitioner can reach tremendous speed in a spin kick and easily knock the opponent unconscious. The strength of the style lies in the practitioner's ability to confuse the adversary.
Eskrima	Close range Filipino fighting art focusing on parries followed by strikes or joint control holds against weak points in an enemy's anatomy, often through the use of a weapon, primarily a stick. Speed is of the essence when seizing the initiative and exploiting an opening. The skilled eskrima fighter not only controls the weapon but takes the enemy down, preventing him from counterattacking.
Haganah	Israeli hand-to-hand integrated combat system focusing on habitual training by limiting practice to a few techniques, bringing the fighter to a point of familiarity under stress. The art's effectiveness is derived from the fact that each technique focuses on achieving a common objective, such as taking an empty-handed opponent to the ground without going down with him, or unarming a weapon-wielding opponent with the intent of restraining, incapacitating, or killing him.

Hap Gar Kung-Fu	A no-nonsense Chinese fighting style several hundred years old with focus on developing power from the waist when striking to damage bones and ligaments. Takedowns and throws are done with full intent on injuring the adversary thus ending the fight. Launching the first strike is stressed rather than reacting to the opponent's attack.
Hapkido	Korean martial art emphasizing ability to flow with opponent's momentum and countering the attack with a takedown or joint lock. Strength advantages are gained by attacking weak points in the adversary's anatomy. The hapkido practitioner must possess good timing to avoid an adversary's attack, and good understanding of human anatomy to effectively apply a lock against a joint. Intercepting the attack and avoiding pitting strength against strength requires full command of evasive movement coupled with aggressive counterattacks.
Hsing-i Chuan	Chinese internal martial art based on five strategic moving patterns developed to help soldiers gain combat proficiency quickly. The hsing-i chuan practitioner uses coordinated movements coupled with sudden bursts of energy and linear footwork when pressing the attack. The art permits no evasive moves prior to counterattack. The ideology behind the art is to shock the enemy into submission.
Hwarang-do	Korean martial art emphasizing a combination of direct and circular moves, and reciprocity of the yin and yang concept. Control of the adversary is achieved through a variety of techniques such as strikes, kicks, joint locks, breaks, and chokes.

Judo	Japanese martial art and combat sport focusing on unbalancing an opponent and taking him to the ground with minimum effort, generally through a dynamic throw. The purpose is to take away the opponent's ability to strike, thus ending the fight. The primary skill of the judoka lies in his ability to time an attack correctly, break the opponent's balance, and move into position to execute a throw while maintaining his own balance.
Kajukenbo	Derived from karate (ka), judo or jujutsu (ju), kenpo (ken), and Chinese boxing (bo), kajukenbo is an American fighting art founded in Hawaii. The kajukenbo practitioner strikes vital targets in preparation for a takedown. A fighter well-versed in kajukenbo might intercept a strike and move forward with aggressive offense forcing the adversary to retreat, and taking him to the ground at the first opportune moment. The kajukenbo practitioner is also skilled at grappling techniques if forced to go to the ground with his opponent.
Karate	Developed in Okinawa, karate exists in many variations, but central to all styles is the ability to deliver a killing or incapacitating blow with power. Karate practitioners focus on defensive blocks and parries followed by offensive strikes and kicks. Hard styles delivering blows in linear fashion differ from soft styles using circular moves.
Kenpo Karate	American kenpo karate emphasizes a continuous flow of motion designed to overwhelm an adversary and unbalance him physically and mentally. Training focuses on keeping the hands in constant motion. The unending flow of blocks, parries, and strikes creates a desired reaction in the opponent. A knife hand strike to the midsection, for example, will draw a reaction that allows the kenpo practitioner to throw a follow-up strike to the throat without a need to reach for the target.

Kickboxing	Originally developed in Japan as an alternative to karate, Western versions of kickboxing have become popular in Europe and the United States. Practitioners of this stand-up fighting art focus on seizing the initiative and pressing the attack with brutal offense aimed at wearing the enemy down and forcing him to retreat. The kickboxer who controls the ring area through footwork and the use of good tactics generally controls the fight and will score favorably with the judges.
Krav Maga	Developed in Israel and involving striking, grabbing, and wrestling techniques, krav maga emphasizes simplicity under stress coupled with a display of confident aggression. Krav maga techniques are based on natural instincts. Fine motor skills and joint locks are used only after the opponent has been neutralized. Techniques that are complex or take a long time to learn are not part of the krav maga practitioner's arsenal.
Kyokushin Karate	This full contact fighting art was developed in Japan by karate master Masutatsu Oyama. Practitioners engage their opponent without the use of gloves or other protective equipment, and each attack is done with full intent of doing damage. Typical techniques include close fist strikes, hand swords, elbow and forearm strikes, and kicks with the knife edge, ball, heel, and instep of the foot. Emphasis is placed on mental conditioning.
Muay Thai	Martial art from Thailand with focus on inflicting maximum damage through the aggressive use of hands, feet, elbows, and knees. The Muay Thai fighter trains for speed, accuracy, and power. Speed allows him to seize the initiative, accuracy enables him to attack the weakest part of the opponent's anatomy with a strong weapon, and power ends the fight.

Ninjutsu	Japanese fighting art relying on stealth and attacks from unpredictable positions and angles. The ninja learns to attack without warning. He is skilled in the use of a large arsenal of traditional and special weapons such as darts, hooks, and blow guns. Ninjutsu practitioners must acquire exceptional physical strength and skill in running, jumping, and swimming.
Pankration	Ancient Greek fighting art displayed in the Greek Olympic Games in 648 BCE. The aim is to defeat the adversary through the use of physical strength coupled with most striking and grappling techniques except biting or eye-gouging. The pankration stylist must be in exceptional physical shape in order to force an often equally strong enemy into submission.
Sambo	Russian martial art evolved from military combat. Sambo encompasses karate style strikes and kicks, judo style takedowns and throws, and jujutsu style arm and leg locks. Its many unorthodox techniques used with full intent of ending the fight quickly made it a versatile combat art and true test of physical and mental tenacity. Many of the techniques involve breaking the opponent's balance while controlling the weapon hand, for example, by kicking or sweeping the opponent's leg or applying a neck takedown.
Sanda	Chinese martial art of free style boxing based on the four tactical elements of punching, kicking, grabbing, and taking the adversary to the ground. The sanda practitioner trains to approach any combat situation with a readiness to kill, as demonstrated in the sanda training regimen which focuses on stamina, physical strength, proficiency in technique, and the acquisition of a mental edge over the adversary.

Savate	French street fighting art, relying primarily on kicks to stop an attacker. A distinguishing characteristic of savate is the use of reinforced shoes similar to wrestling shoes. Geared toward full contact fighting with focus on hard training and sparring, savate is unique among street fighting styles. The savate practitioner's emphasis on techniques considered essential in street fights, while ignoring forms practice and spirituality, makes him a tough opponent in a battle that has as its goal to incapacitate the enemy.
Shaolin Kung-Fu	A collection of martial arts associated with the Shaolin Monastery in China. The shaolin kung-fu practitioner dedicates his life to the purpose of kung-fu. He is skilled in several combat maneuvers, but favors a few specific hand, foot, or weapon techniques, which he will master to perfection. Central to shaolin kung-fu is a strong stance that allows the practitioner to withstand the power of an attack.
Shotokan Karate	Japanese hard style with roots in Okinawa characterized by deep stances and powerful strikes through linear moves and determined offense. The shotokan karate practitioner relies mainly on straight strikes and kicks with full bodyweight behind the blows. Circling the opponent is done mainly as a diversion. When it is time to attack, it is done with the purpose of "killing" or ending the fight with a single blow.
Small Circle Jujitsu	American martial art developed in Hawaii but with roots in ancient Japanese jujutsu. Practitioners focus on flow and economy of motion, and on mastering transitions from one technique to another. Success depends on exerting continuous pain, communicating to the adversary that a break or joint dislocation is imminent.

Sumo	Japanese wrestling art relying on size and strength over finesse with the aim of unbalancing a lighter or less skilled opponent and forcing him out of the ring. Sumo was traditionally developed with the goal of slaying the adversary through the use of maximum force. The sumo wrestler focuses on growing his body as large as possible in order to gain the power to outmuscle an adversary.
Taekwondo	Korean martial art with strong focus on kicks, although hand techniques remain part of the art. Since kicks are his primary weapon, the taekwondo practitioner must be particularly watchful of guarding his legs, which, if damaged, will destroy his fighting capacity. The taekwondo practitioner must develop exceptional strength, speed, and flexibility. A taekwondo kick delivered with speed and precision has the capacity to end a fight instantly.
Wing Chun Kung-Fu	Chinese martial art with focus on the use of penetrating force acquired through overpowering aggression, simplicity of movement, shortest distance to the target, simultaneous offense and defense, and precise positioning and body mechanics. Designed to benefit the smaller or weaker fighter, the wing chun practitioner remains in contact with his opponent throughout the altercation. The moment the distance increases, he closes the gap, presses the attack, and launches an array of straight strikes along his centerline.

A difference between Sun Tzu and Clausewitz is that Sun Tzu wrote his book as a roadmap to success by stating in clear language the types of strategies and tactics the victorious army uses. The most commonly repeated advice might be, "Know your enemy and know yourself, and in a hundred battles you will never be in peril." Clausewitz, by contrast, did not give specific advice on how to behave, but recognized the many uncertainties of war through his theory of "friction." The principles discussed in Sun Tzu's and Clausewitz's books—seizing the initiative, imposing your will on the

Capoeira stylists practicing their art in the streets. Understanding the essence of your martial art will assist you in decreasing the risk of failure. The strength of capoeira lies in the practitioner's ability to evade an attack and counter with elusive sweeps or head kicks. *(Image source: Aroma De Limon, Wikimedia Commons)*

enemy, destroying his forces, correct use of defense, etc.—do not apply to any particular martial art per se. As discussed in chapter 1, the nature of fighting remains constant regardless of the art you study or the tactics (techniques) you use to defeat the adversary. Although scientific analysis of combat is necessary to broaden one's understanding, determine an attacker's motive, and learn the fashion in which he might attack, Sun Tzu and Clausewitz agreed that war is essentially an art and not a science. Success in war requires an ability to adapt and use artistic expression derived from much study and practice. Knowing your enemy and yourself is excellent advice. However, as Clausewitz reminded us, acting properly upon that knowledge is more difficult. As further reinforced by the ancient Chinese classic, *The Methods of the Ssu-Ma*, "It is not knowing what to do that is difficult; it is putting it into effect that is hard."[9]

CHAPTER 9

MORAL QUALITY OF COURAGE

"If a general is not courageous, he will be unable to conquer doubts or to create great plans." — **Sun Tzu**

"With uncertainty in one scale, courage and self-confidence must be thrown into the other to correct the balance." — **Carl von Clausewitz**

In face of threat, the first moral quality is courage. But since the human mind is typically more attracted to uncertainty than certainty, individual combatants tend to be unsure of their capabilities and unable to act with confidence. Good training instills the courage to face an opponent in battle and handle the various pains of combat: physical injury, fatigue, fear, and uncertainty. Courage takes two forms: acting resolutely and making major decisions responsibly when faced with personal danger. Boldness as an element of courage is based on strong situational awareness and tends to increase as a result of success, but must be tempered with judgment. The courageous combatant is therefore steadfast in battle, but employs forethought and intellect to avoid falling victim to impulsive or reckless actions that may ultimately lead to his downfall.

Although determination can balance the playing field for he who lacks physical size or strength, injury or public humiliation may prevent the martial artist from sustaining a high degree of courage for the duration of a fight. Knowing your enemy and yourself, as explained in chapter 8, will open the road to victory but also requires an ability to instill fear in the enemy. Comprehension of the enemy's strategy and the capacity to convince him that potential harm may come his way will likely make him reluctant to meet you in battle. The ancient Chinese texts underscored the importance of creating a strategic position that will ultimately undermine and demoralize the enemy, or as Sun Tzu said, "[T]hose skilled in warfare move the enemy, and are not moved by the enemy."[1] Simultaneously, battle seldom goes down as originally envisioned. However, proper preparation, as reflected in the concept of ch'i, gives the soldier and martial artist the confidence he needs to fight courageously.

Since war is danger, Carl von Clausewitz agreed that the first quality the fighter must possess is courage. "War is the province of physical exertion and suffering," he said. "In order not to be completely overcome by them, a certain strength of body and mind is required."[2] Courage involves the physical ability to engage an enemy in battle when one fully knows that one may get hurt or killed. In the martial arts, physical courage relates to the particular tactics the martial artist uses based on his strength and stamina or flexibility. If he lacks physical strength, he would rely on deception rather than insisting on meeting the enemy in pitched battle. If he lacks flexibility in the legs, he would kick low or not at all rather than attempting to kick to the head. Moral courage, by contrast, relates to mental resolve and ability to make an informed decision about the benefits of fighting. It involves boldness and daring, and as such must be tempered by judgment and self-control. Since the consequence of recklessness is injury or death, an effort to calculate the likelihood of emerging victorious must be made prior to entering battle. As explored in previous chapters, one should enter the fight from a position of strength whenever possible.

Clausewitz further believed that since each person possesses a different set of emotional qualities, it is exceedingly difficult to construct a universally valid theory for action. For example, some martial artists believe that the soft martial arts suit their personality traits better than the hard arts, and vice versa. Other factors such as the particular moment one decides to revert from defense to offense might differ between individuals, even in theoretically identical combat situations. Since combat is a product of human beings, it consists of the human emotions of anger, fear, excitement, and even joy. The answer to such questions as whether or not you should give a potential attacker your wallet when he asks for it, or fight him in physical battle instead, is therefore not immediately apparent. The moral factors of experience, morale, and intuition tend to affect war making as much as friction and chance.

This chapter examines the effects of courage on fighting and the emotional factors involved in rousing a person to action. It discusses the need for a balanced perspective between boldness and intellect to ensure the best possible outcome.

Key Points: Moral Quality of Courage

Sun Tzu	Carl von Clausewitz
Soldiers can be motivated to fight through personal rewards.	Courage is the primary quality needed to face danger and is achieved through pride and excitement.
Creating a strategic position that will undermine the enemy's courage is crucial to success.	Boldness comes through confidence and from the weakness of others.
Emotions can rouse soldiers to action.	Spirit is the driving force behind courageous action.
Hasty decisions based on emotions result in impaired judgment and recklessness.	Boldness must be guided by intellect.

What is courage? Clausewitz described physical courage as "courage in presence of danger to the person," and moral courage as "courage before responsibility."[3] Acts rooted in fear are generally associated with the physical preservation of one's being and also involve escape from danger. Acts rooted in courage, by contrast, are associated with the moral preservation of one's being (one's reputation) and require a willingness to face an enemy in battle even when options exist for walking away.

Since war involves combat, and combat involves the physical destruction of the enemy forces and the defense of one's own, it naturally follows that war is dangerous. Courage may therefore be the most significant of the so-called moral qualities. Moral courage is influenced by pride, patriotism, and enthusiasm, which can rouse a person to action and sometimes to recklessness and lack of judgment. Consider a martial artist tempted to show off his skills to his friends when confronted by a bully on the street. Or, as another example, consider somebody insulting your girlfriend in a bar. Would you feel obliged, as a matter of pride, to come to her defense even as you know intellectually that the better choice is to leave the bar quietly, or perhaps even offer an apology to the offender for the sake of keeping the peace? Pride, as the driving force behind action, can lead you down a path that ultimately results in physical injury to all parties involved.

Clausewitz further reminded us that "war is the province of chance," and one cannot know with certainty whether or not one's actions will preserve one's safety or result in even greater physical danger.[4] Learning to control the type of courage that stems from pride and enthusiasm may therefore be particularly crucial. Many martial arts teach us that he who turns his back on conflict and walks away has courage. Since people love winners and walking away implies cowardice, it does indeed require tremendous moral courage (that of good judgment) to walk away from a potential fight, particularly if the masses are watching. However, differences of opinion exist also on this issue. While Plato, a Greek philosopher of the fifth to fourth centuries BCE, defined courage as "the virtue of fleeing from an inevitable danger,"[5] the Greek historian Polybius expressed in the second century BCE that soldiers regarded "their one supreme duty not to flee or leave the ranks," and were "expected never to surrender or be captured."[6]

Even if one has found peace with the decision to walk away, difficulties may arise because circumstances often demand immediate action. In other words, the opportunity to think about what to do and how to act (or not act) is simply not available. The training the martial artist receives is in part intended to help him determine which situations are worth defending with physical action and which require a more modest approach to ensure the best possible outcome. The deeper meaning of the words courtesy and self-control are worth exploring. For example, how far should you go with respect to courtesy if the favor is not returned? How much self-control should you have when your sparring partner hits too hard and bringing the matter to his attention verbally has no effect?

Moral courage is also about standing up for one's beliefs. The difficulty lies in knowing where to draw the line. Fighters are often seen losing their temper in competition. Remember when Mike Tyson bit off Evander Holyfield's ear in a boxing bout in 1997? Martial artists have hopefully received more training in controlling

Maintaining composure and avoiding reckless actions when taking an unexpected kick to the head requires boldness coupled with intellect. *(Image source: Indrek Galetin, Wikimedia Commons)*

their tempers, but it is still common for emotions to flare. Consider what kind of reputation you would like to preserve for yourself, and how you can best achieve this. Your answer might help guide your actions. Furthermore, since we have a tendency "in momentary emergencies" to be "swayed more by feelings than thoughts,"[7] it is prudent to rehearse the scenarios one can expect to encounter beforehand. Strategic planning brings strength of soul and resoluteness in action. A fight is typically thought as having begun when the first strike is thrown or the first move is made with the intent of throwing a strike or kick. But the skilled martial artist understands that fights begin in the mind long before the first blows are exchanged, and that a person's intentions are often revealed through his facial expressions or general demeanor. A skilled opponent can therefore preempt any sudden move you make. When faced with an attentive enemy, you must be particularly watchful of your emotions and avoid signaling your intentions.

Like Clausewitz, who believed that pride and enthusiasm can prompt a person to act, Sun Tzu was quick to note the effects of emotions on the soldier. Soldiers, he said, are made "courageous in overcoming the enemy" by rousing them to anger.[8] Like Clausewitz, he stressed that hasty decisions based on emotions rather than judgment often result in recklessness. It is better to withdraw from a challenge if possible, than to give way to the temptation to appear courageous in front of one's peers and fight a battle that one cannot win: "If weaker numerically, be capable of withdrawing. And if in all respects unequal, be capable of eluding him [the enemy], for a small force is but booty for one more powerful if it fights recklessly."[9] Good judgment further necessitates that victory be sought but not be demanded by others. As Sun Tzu reminded us, "When the enemy presents an opportunity, [one should] speedily take advantage of it. Seize the place which the enemy values without making an appointment for battle with him."[10]

Furthermore, a balance must be struck between compassion and rage. As Sun Tzu warned us, there are five qualities which are fatal in the character of a general (or, if applied to the martial arts, in the character of a martial artist). Consider the words so many of us repeat in the training hall: modesty, courtesy, integrity, self-control, perseverance, indomitable spirit. The martial artist, if reckless, can be killed; "if cowardly, captured; if quick-tempered, he can be provoked to rage and make a fool of himself; if he has too delicate a sense of honor, he can be easily insulted; if he is of a compassionate nature, you can harass him."[11] Thus, "[i]f you are not in danger, do not fight a war. For while an angered man may again be happy, and a resentful man again be pleased, a state that has perished cannot be restored, nor can the dead be brought back to life."[12]

As can be deduced from these writings, the significance of the moral forces rests with the fact that it is from these that fighting spirit, the driving force behind combat, is derived. When a combatant loses his desire to carry on the battle, even if his physical forces are intact, all preplanned strategy and tactics will fall by the wayside and he will accept defeat. Victory certainly fuels the fighting spirit, but a martial artist's true test of courage may come when he enters battle or competition willingly after having lost several fights

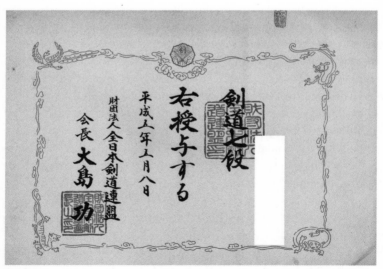

Belts and certificates honoring achievements can build a martial artist's courage and act as motivators for continued training. *(Image source: Yappakoredesho, Wikimedia Commons)*

in a row, knowing that the audience is rooting for his opponent. Although it takes extraordinary courage to overcome this reluctance to battle from the position of the underdog, it is not the same type of courage required in the defense of life. As Clausewitz reminded us, "If a young man to show his skill in horsemanship leaps across a deep cleft, then he is bold; if he makes the same leap pursued by a troop of head-chopping Janissaries [soldiers in a former elite Turkish guard] he is only resolute."[13] Thus, the difference between moral and physical courage, and why soldiers can be motivated to fight based on the promise of personal rewards for their accomplishments. "When you plunder the countryside," Sun Tzu suggested, "divide the wealth among your troops."[14] Motivational rewards in the martial arts come in the form of trophies and belts, which translate into higher status in the training hall. Moral attributes such as wisdom, benevolence, and courage can further earn a martial artist his enemy's respect. "Those who excel in war," Sun Tzu said, "first cultivate their humanity and maintain their laws and institutions."[15]

Along with proper etiquette comes the observance of a set of disciplined rituals, such as introducing oneself before battle or bowing to the opponent, which are meant to radiate confidence and possibly deter a potential attacker. The bow before battle is also an honorary gesture to the generations of warriors who have built the fighting arts. As explained by one master tang soo do practitioner, every bow is "a tribute to all the people who spent countless hours training and refining the art so we, their descendents, would have something of value."[16] China's historical battles speak of how rituals gave the soldiers confidence while simultaneously instilling fear in the adversary. In the Spring and Autumn period (c. 722-481 BCE), "when the lord of Chin was advancing to attack the state of Ch'i," the advancing general established outposts in the mountains and set out flags even in places where his army did not intend to go. The ritual communicated strength and confidence, which ultimately caused the enemy to flee.[17] As reinforced by historian Victor Davis Hanson in his evaluation of ancient Greek warfare, "Conflict is often irrational in nature and more a result of strong emotions than of material need… War is sometimes won or lost as much by confidence in one's culture as by military assets themselves."[18]

However, while a martial artist may investigate and learn about the opponent's physical capacity before battle, knowing his mental strength is more difficult. A martial artist of small stature may be targeted by a bigger person because he invokes the impression that his physical strength is inadequate. A small person must therefore demonstrate that he is unwilling to be a victim. By the same token, a person who is physically strong can be beaten if his will to fight is destroyed, for example, through fear. All one has to do is listen to some prefight interviews to learn about how full-contact fighters attempt to psych themselves up for the fight. Consider also the ring names they choose: Scorpion, Hammer, Rest in Peace, Battle Axe, etc.

Although war is about life and death, the greatest battle you fight may be the one within you. *Hagakure: The Book of the Samurai* by Yamamoto Tsunetomo focuses on how to develop the mental attitude necessary to face combat, and how to die gracefully and fearlessly. The samurai could fight with intensity because they faced the possibility of death daily and had been conditioned to believe it a disgrace "to die with a weapon yet undrawn."[19] From a practical military standpoint, letting go of all hope of winning allows one to enter the fight with maximum strength and focus. Embracing death, not even hoping to live, erases all regret and creates a fearsome warrior. Clausewitz agreed that boldness to proceed comes through confidence, but also "from the weakness of others."[20] Whenever a contestant performs poorly in a sparring match or martial arts competition, the confidence of his opponents tends to grow. Likewise, a contestant who performs brilliantly can cause loss of confidence in others and hinder their ability to demonstrate their skills as flawlessly as hoped. But boldness neither constitutes heroism, nor should be a "blind outburst of passion to no purpose."[21] To remain effective, it must be coupled with a reflective mind. Reenacting a fight in the training hall the way one might experience it on the battlefield will help one understand the difficulties associated with a preplanned attack.

In sports competition, for example, your plan might be to take control of the fight as soon as the bell signals the start of the first round and systematically press the attack, when your opponent foils your plans only seconds into the round by landing a strike that sets your head spinning. Are your moral forces still intact, or does the blood dripping on the canvas fuel a feeling of physical and mental inferiority? In the midst of confusion, moving to action requires emotional stability, mental endurance, and an ability to know how to use the means at your disposal. It is a well-known fact that fine motor skills tend to deteriorate when a person is under stress to defend his life or well-being. This is one reason why many of the so-called reality based martial arts rely on techniques that are relatively simple to learn and use gross rather than fine motor skills. Punches and most kicks fall into the category of gross motor skills because they are drawn from intuition and rely on moves that a small child can do naturally. Wrist locks, by contrast, rely on fine motor skills because they are not intuitive but must be learned and

As demonstrated by these sailors, gross motor skills, generally associated with punching and kicking, prove invaluable when trying to adjust to the chaos and uncertainty of the battlefield and will aid one in keeping one's moral forces intact. (*Image source: Joseph Lomangino, Wikimedia Commons*)

require considerable precision to execute with success. Krav maga aims at making effective combatants within a few months of training. The same cannot be said for aikido, which may take a lifetime to learn with proficiency.[22]

Even martial artists who have endured years of training tend to revert to the natural instinctive moves of punching and kicking when taken by surprise in a threat to their life or safety. To gain the most from training, the martial artist can study the raw instinctive move of a punch or kick, and then make small adjustments to increase the power and finesse of the technique, thereby raising his confidence. Practitioners of hap gar kung-fu (see also hop gar kung-fu), a no-nonsense Chinese fighting style several hundred years old, do just this, for example, by learning how to develop power from the waist while striking with simple punches that come naturally. The style retains its combat roots by focusing on damaging blows to bones and ligaments rather than on submission techniques. Takedowns and throws are done with as much force as possible and with full intent on injuring the adversary and ending the fight. The hap gar fighter tries to avoid going to the ground with his opponent. Direct attacks to vital targets—eyes, throat, groin—are emphasized, as is launching the first strike rather than reacting to the opponent's attack. All techniques and forms are practiced as a means to an end with focus on moves that are intuitive and natural to perform by the human body, and as such contribute to the strength of one's moral forces.[23]

The difficulties of acting with precision when one's life is threatened can be offset in part by following a solid and orderly plan that brings familiarity to combat. He who faces the chaos of battle, Clausewitz writes, "must be a very extraordinary man who, under these impressions for the first time, does not lose the power of making any instantaneous decisions."[24] Sun Tzu likewise underscored the importance of order: "The battlefield may seem in confusion and chaos, but one's array must be in good order. That will be proof against defeat."[25] Thus, as discussed in chapter 3, something should be said for habitual training, since familiarity with danger is necessary in order to produce the kind of calculated courage a person needs to swing the odds in his favor. Forms practice, although considered by some as nearly useless in the contemporary world, offers a wealth of discipline and self-control which is essential to developing boldness guided by intellect. Learning a new form is in itself a test of commitment and patience. Improving the movements in the form takes additional discipline. Forms practice helps the martial artist establish a sound mental strength foundation for continued study. Practicing a form hundreds of times also conditions the body to the strains of combat and assists muscle memory, making responses to threats more natural.

Furthermore, perseverance without losing one's bearings when under heavy attack, and an ability to stop negative thoughts and imaginary fears from interfering, requires that one views battle from a logical perspective. The combat arts thus demand continuous training and effort to create a mental state at which the martial artist can act responsibly, unobstructed by emotions and without excessive thought. *Zanshin*, a term used in the Japanese martial arts to indicate awareness, is achieved through experience and produces a state of detachment in threatening situations, which further allows the practitioner to gain perspective on the situation and prevent emotions from interfering with sound judgment.[26] Aikido practitioners tend to understand this concept quite well. Superior self-control allows the aikidoka to blend his strength with the opponent's, all the while foregoing egotistical tendencies aimed at double-weightedness, or the clashing of one's yang force with the opponent's. The martial genius, as Clausewitz said, sees a guiding light in a cluttered environment. By contrast, he who lacks the moral quality of courage will be unable to command his forces or set his plans into action.

Going forth into battle with resoluteness and courage is thus a choice made after careful deliberation and analysis. Consider these words by the ancient Greek historian, Thucydides: "For no man comes to execute a thing with the same confidence he premeditates it. For we deliver opinions in safety, whereas in the action itself we fail through fear."[27] A trained martial artist is slow to anger and chooses his battles carefully. He ponders the dangers before taking action and does not accept a challenge based on an insult. He might have learned to press the attack, yet continuing along the current path after suffering a number of setbacks would indicate recklessness. When the strategy is faulty because the opponent is too strong or too aggressive, the tactics, the blows one uses to press the attack, will not secure the objective, which is why the most courageous action may well be to walk away while the option still exists.

Although both victors and vanquished will experience losses in war, strategic and tactical superiority coupled with courage increase the martial artist's chances of success. Sun Tzu reminded us that when on "difficult ground, press on; in encircled ground, devise stratagems, in desperate ground, fight courageously."[28] If the fight is difficult, press forward to get through the difficulties as quickly as possible; if the enemy is numerically superior or physically stronger, look for a tactical advantage; if your life is directly threatened, there may be no choice but to fight with all the courage of your being, win or lose. However, although Sun Tzu emphasized calculated risk and Clausewitz preferred boldness in attack, a balance must be struck between caution and boldness. Caution does not imply timidity or cowardice. In fact, "deliberate caution," Clausewitz noted, "may be considered bold in its own right and is certainly just as powerful and effective [as boldness]."[29] A revealing example of caution coupled with boldness might be found in iaijutsu, or the military art of drawing the sword without telegraphing one's intent to the opponent. Prepared to confront danger at any moment by taking advantage of tactical surprise, the Japanese swordsman exercised tremendous patience and self-control while waiting for the perfect moment to seize the initiative and defeat the enemy with a single swift cut with the sword.

How does one prevent cowardice from gaining a foothold within oneself? According to Sun Tzu, you start by prohibiting "superstitious doubts." When you "do away with rumors; then nobody will flee even in death."[30] We have thus come full circle back to what may have been Sun Tzu's most famous dictum: Know your enemy and yourself. Uncertainty brings fear. Start by striving to understand the enemy's needs and how far he is willing to go to secure them.

Also understand your own ability and needs and how far you are willing to go to protect them. When you know your enemy and yourself, you will project an air of confidence which may halt the enemy's advance. In the training hall, practice the projection of your voice; learn how to say a definite no when you mean to say a definite no. The fact that many martial arts schools stress "indomitable spirit" is further testimony to the importance of strong morals in war. Next time you participate in a competition or martial arts demonstration, note how those who act as if they own the arena will draw higher scores than those who enter the competition with an uncertain or timid demeanor. The bold student may not be a better martial artist per se than his more timid counterpart, but the projection of passion and fighting spirit will communicate that he is and may swing the odds in his favor.

Thus, the power to act in the martial arts comes not only through physical strength and stamina, but from passion and ability to exercise command presence, which is further a result of having deep knowledge of your enemy, yourself, and the environment. Kung-fu grandmaster Don Baird notes how you can strike and kick a 300-pound bag in the training hall or spar with your peers and maintain full confidence in your abilities. But when you enter a different environment, when you no longer wear the familiar clothing of a martial artist, when all the faces have changed, you will suddenly feel small. To build command presence even in unfamiliar places, Baird recommends training in the wilderness where you can project your power beyond yourself and the familiarity of the dojo. "I felt so small and insignificant," recalls Baird. "A single punch, even a shout, seemed like nothing while standing in the midst of Angeles National Forest."[31] When you return to the arena of your school after such an experience, you will feel much bigger than before.

As demonstrated in this chapter, moral factors include individual personality traits such as courage and passion. How one responds to a threat is due partly to learned habits as a result of training, and partly to one's natural inclinations and enthusiasm. Students who come to class by their own choice will generally outlast those who are motivated to come by others (children, for example, whose par-

This statue of Kano Jigoro (1860-1938 CE), the founder of judo, outside the Kodo-kan Institute in Tokyo, Japan, stands as a reminder of the dedication and spirit re-quired to understand combat and master a martial art. *(Image source: Henrik Probell, Wikimedia Commons)*

ents send them to class against their wishes). Those who have a natural passion for the martial arts will also spend more time in training away from the dojo and will generally excel over those whose motivation stems from outside factors. Personal motivation is one reason why it is difficult to predict the outcome of a fight based only on a person's length of training or how many techniques he knows.

Furthermore, he who lacks passion for the martial arts will also lack creativity and fail to make the best use of the techniques he knows. Spending time outside of class, analyzing techniques and experimenting with concepts rather than simply memorizing sequences of moves, is invaluable for he who wants to excel in the combat environment. As we have learned, war is both a science and an art and pure memorization without creativity will make you fall victim to chance the moment the first "shots" are fired and your plans fall apart. As Clausewitz said, "Military activity is never directed against material force alone; it is always aimed simultaneously at the moral forces which give it life."[32]

The time you spend in the training hall will lay the cornerstone for your martial arts journey; it is where you grow as a martial artist, build courage by learning about and experiencing the different elements of combat, contemplate yourself and your enemies, and find peace with your decision. Individual creativity and the moral elements of courage, willpower, and enthusiasm will fill the gaps and make the journey whole. He who is rightly prepared thus has the confidence to meet his fate in battle.

CHAPTER 10

SECURING VICTORY

"Victory is the main objective in war."   — Sun Tzu

"The immediate object of an attack is victory."
                              — Carl von Clausewitz

Victory is secured in three ways: by depriving the enemy of physical strength through death or wounds; by destroying his morale and fighting spirit; and by convincing him that the battle is not worth fighting. Although friction affects the outcome of battle, victory or defeat are not merely random happenings. You can do several things to improve your chances of emerging victorious. First, the better fighter tends to win. Who is "better"? Generally, he who has prepared well and displays a strong physical and mental resolve is the better fighter. Second, although friction can interfere with the best-laid plans, fighters who have prepared thoroughly will have a back-up plan that can minimize the effects of friction. Third, the physically strong and mentally prepared fighter can change his plans midstream to offset at least some of the effects of friction.[1]

Sun Tzu belonged to the school of Daoism. With respect to warfare, the ultimate goal was to restore the "cosmic harmony" through the use of the least amount of force possible. "All warfare," he meant, "is based [less on strength than] on deceit." Rather than fighting a pitched battle, one should confuse the enemy in order to weaken him. While force was not placed at the center of Sun Tzu's war strategy, perhaps even more significant is the insight that the need to fight is itself an indication that one is in disharmony with the cosmic order and the perfect state of existence.[2] Victory is thus attained by placing the enemy in a state of mental confusion and chaos. According to the *Wei Liao-Tzu*, an ancient Chinese military text, victory is gained by causing the enemy's ch'i (spirit) to be lost and his forces to scatter.[3]

However, it is equally true that when two combatants collide in battle, the fighter who can use physical strength and size to his advantage is likely to win. As discussed previously, the art of pankration, or the game of "All Powers," an all-encompassing system of fighting developed in ancient Greece, relies on physical strength and power over finesse and combines elements of boxing and wrestling. Techniques that do not demonstrate physical strength, such as biting and eye-gouging, are considered dishonorable. Pankrationists therefore have to be in superb physical shape (size is a plus) in order to secure victory through knockout or submission. Throughout the fight, they are left with the crucial decision of selecting the precise target that will end the match. The strategy (the combat plan) and the tactics (the specific techniques used to ensure victory) depend on each combatant's ability to properly identify the opponent's center of gravity (his strength, but also his critical point of vulnerability). The pankrationist uses judgment to create a situation that favors physical force.

Although one individual fighter may be better than another, questions about the alleged superiority (or the value) of one martial art over another are difficult to answer without considering the historical context under which the various fighting arts were developed. Understanding how victory is determined therefore requires a critical study of Asian and Western strategy and tactics. Whether or not you are able to claim the victory also depends on your relative superiority. You can win because you are strong, but you can also win because the opponent is weak. Had you fought on any other day against any other fighter, the outcome may well have proven less advantageous. According to Carl von Clausewitz, victory can be made more honorable by mentioning the difficulties you encountered along the way, but defeat does not become less disgraceful by bringing into light the many difficulties.[4]

So what is the role of physical skill in battle, and how does one determine if a martial artist is truly skillful? Is victory necessarily reliant upon skill or does it depend mainly on the circumstances surrounding the contest? Although in favor of conquering an enemy "already defeated," Sun Tzu understood that the "expert" is not he who does the ordinary: "To foresee a victory which the ordinary man can foresee is not the acme of excellence . . . to distinguish between the sun and the moon is no test of vision, to hear the thunderclap is no indication of acute hearing."[5] The expert martial artist has a firm grasp of the underlying principles of battle; he is a good strategist as well as tactician. He can control the enemy, impose his will on him, and avoid fighting from an inferior position directly in the enemy's line of power.

This chapter discusses the elements that will assist one's pursuit of victory in reference to the concepts and principles that have been presented throughout this book, to include numerical superiority, destruction of the enemy force, and sound defensive practices. The importance of winning, the moral qualities required to achieve a lasting victory, and the preservation of peace are also considered.

Key Points: Securing Victory

Sun Tzu	Carl von Clausewitz
Deceptive practices are superior to physical strength.	Create a situation that favors the use of physical force.
Losses prove heavy even for victors. Seek a quick victory by conquering "an enemy already defeated."	Establish the laws of war by seizing the initiative and introducing the elements of war.
Numerical superiority is achieved by dividing the enemy forces.	Numerical superiority most commonly decides the victory.
Victory is achieved only when the enemy accepts defeat.	Victory is achieved when the political objective is achieved.

Sun Tzu underscored the importance conquering "an enemy already defeated."[6] A martial artist who cannot avoid the fight altogether might attempt to defeat the opponent mentally rather than physically. Although a mental defeat can involve the use of diplomatic negotiations, this does not necessarily have to be the case. One can also use a convincing display of force to frighten the enemy into submission before blows are physically exchanged. The martial artist can practice this principle by demonstrating techniques or forms in front of a critical audience, thereby robbing any competitors of their confidence. Although cunning, surprise, and avoidance of pitched battle pitting strength against strength increase one's chances of emerging victorious particularly when fighting an enemy that is numerically superior, note that Sun Tzu was not against the use of physical force per se. He recognized that "war was a matter of vital importance to the state; a recourse to be undertaken when other means have failed. Sun Tzu's view of the army as 'an instrument to deliver the coup de grace to an enemy made vulnerable by stratagem and deception,' appears repeatedly in Chinese history."[7]

Clausewitz, although focusing on the use of physical force, agreed with Sun Tzu that "the side that first introduces the element of war [through a display of force, for example] is also the side that establishes the initial laws of war,"[8] and that this may ease one's pursuit of victory or possibly lead to the avoidance of battle. For example, a martial artist who is the first contestant to enter a forms competition and whose performance is outstanding will raise the bar and thus establish "the initial laws of war" for subsequent competitors, who may have trouble outperforming him even when highly skilled.

Once Sun Tzu and Clausewitz had laid down their respective theories for success, both agreed that numerical superiority is of utmost importance, that attacking the decisive point gives one a relative strength advantage and shortens the duration of battle, and that positioning and proper use of the environment will swing the odds in one's favor. To properly apply these ideas, the martial artist must develop a combat plan based on intimate familiarity with oneself and knowledge of the opponent's strengths and weaknesses.

A fighter whose strengths are takedowns and submission holds must overcome the challenge of closing the distance, and must understand his opponent's strengths and weaknesses to score a victory. A relative strength advantage can be gained through superior positioning that allows one to attack the opponent's balance, as demonstrated in this choke/neck takedown. (*Image source: Doug Meil, Wikimedia Commons*)

Physical strength is a key factor deciding the victory, or as Clausewitz said, "In tactics as in strategy, superiority of numbers is the most common element in victory."[9] Since numerical superiority is so beneficial, the martial artist must not only prepare for the confrontation by building physical strength, but must be well-versed in the techniques of his art in order to offer a formidable resistance against a much stronger enemy. Sun Tzu recognized that numerical superiority can either be factual or perceived and is achieved, for example, by dividing the enemy's strength. The martial artist can utilize this principle by attacking high and low targets in rapid succession and forcing the enemy to defend several critical points simultaneously. Options for dividing the enemy's strength include attacking weak points in the anatomy (eyes, throat, groin, joints) from unexpected angles, or upsetting the adversary's mental state

by attacking his balance. Furthermore, control of the combat arena, and proper positioning away from the opponent's line of power
through footwork and movement, enables the martial artist to
avoid a head-on clash pitting strength against strength.

Before entering battle, you must know that the advantage rests
with you. Common sense plays a role, which is why we seldom see
a small person initiating an attack against a much bigger person, or
a single man taking on several opponents in hand-to-hand combat
by choice. When you have done your prefight planning and determined that you do not have the physical strength or ability to attack the decisive point, nor the ability to use superior positioning
or surprise and deception, the better option may be avoiding battle
altogether. Many Asian martial arts advocate honor and integrity
over winning at all cost. A fighting art's method of employment
contributes to how it is perceived. One might ask then, does the
end justify the means? Sun Tzu underscored that battle should never be taken lightly. Due to its great destructive capabilities, heavy
losses are likely even for victors. Whether or not one chooses to
use force depends on calculations of relative power. To minimize
losses, war should be viewed rationally rather than emotionally, as
reflected in his statement that, "[a] government should not mobilize an army out of anger, military leaders should not provoke war
out of wrath."[10] Personal combat should be viewed no less critical
and be approached in the same way. When emotions flare, fights
erupt. Thus, the better option is to avoid battle if possible, not out
of compassion for the enemy, but to preserve life.

Popular martial arts further suggest that the reason why we learn
to fight is so that we do not have to fight. To ease the way to victory, Sun Tzu warned us not to press an enemy that is cornered,
but to "leave an outlet," a gate to life.[11] Humiliation can prompt
an adversary to fight to the death even in a hopeless situation. As
military historian Victor Davis Hanson writes about the World War
II battles on Okinawa:

> Americans were convinced that Asians in general did not
> value life—theirs or anyone else's—in the same manner

as Westerners, and when faced with overwhelming military power and sure defeat would nevertheless continue to fight hard . . . The Japanese quit on Okinawa when they were killed off, not when the fall of a particular ridge or line of defenses forecast eventual tactical defeat . . . War ended when the enemy was exterminated or faced with certain annihilation. It did not necessarily stop when the Japanese were encircled, outmaneuvered, or shorn of supplies.[12]

Sun Tzu further advocated weighing the risks carefully before entering battle and considering the benefits that victory will bring, as demonstrated through his statement, "[I]f there is no gain, do not use troops."[13] This is a reminder to the martial artist that his is an activity that deals in the reality of combat and therefore in life and death, and that he must use his power judiciously. Furthermore, when the victor is gracious, better future relations can be ensured between the parties. *Guanxi*, emphasized in Confucian doctrine, is a relationship of trust and general awareness of the needs between two people, and through which balance and harmony is achieved and hostilities are calmed. However, it might be worth noting that harmony can generally not endure "without a sense of obeisance from the weaker partner."[14] From a practical viewpoint, the idea of leaving the enemy an out and not humiliating him in defeat is important only because it is aimed at creating a lasting victory by discouraging him from returning with a vengeance. It does not mean that one should avoid using full force when one's life is threatened. Do not assume that an enemy who is neutralized momentarily will leave you alone if given the chance to replenish his forces and rise again.

Sometimes victory can lead to intoxication with success and overconfidence in future battles, and may prevent one from conducting a proper examination of the enemy and oneself. The martial arts typically teach adherence to a policy of humility. A martial artist who avoids bragging about his accomplishments and lets his skill speak for itself decreases the risk of underestimating the opponent's skill or overestimating his own. Since he can never fully prepare for the effects of friction, physical and mental preparation must be a continuous effort based on realistic expectations. When examining war critically, examining the means employed and not just the end result seems like a valid suggestion. However, in the pursuit of victory, a particular means "is not fairly open to censure," according to Clausewitz, "until a better is pointed out."[15] Victory is achieved only when the enemy accepts defeat. Thus, ultimately, only the end result matters.

Furthermore, stability in conflict is seldom achieved in full and in agreement with the victor's terms, which illustrates the meaning of Clausewitz's statement that "in war the result is never final" but merely a transitory evil for the defeated power.[16] If you win a kickboxing match today but are challenged to a rematch tomorrow, the outcome may not be in your favor. You may protect yourself against theft today, but be taken by surprise tomorrow. Thus, a "military victory" today does not guarantee a lasting victory tomorrow. You might also experience a so-called Pyrrhic victory (relating to the staggering losses that King Pyrrhus of Epirus, a Greek general of the Hellenistic era, took when defeating the Romans in 280 and 279 BCE) by winning in theory, yet walking away with losses so heavy that you wonder if the battle was worth fighting at all. This is yet a reason why one should not take war lightly or enter battle carelessly.

Although defense is the stronger form of war, both Sun Tzu and Clausewitz understood that victory lies in the attack. As discussed in chapter 7, the purpose of defense is to await an opportunity to attack an enemy who has been weakened by time. But perpetual defense cannot win the war. You must take action at some point. Battle, according to Clausewitz, "is a conflict waged with all our forces for the attainment of a decisive victory."[17] This statement demonstrates his concern with the effectiveness of battle and not with its ethics or morality. He did not view physical conflict in terms of "a search for truth or justice but only as a struggle of wills."[18] The best fighter is not he who adheres to the greatest morals, but he who wins.[19]

Sun Tzu took no less of a pragmatic approach to battle. He believed that "one who knows how to use both large and small forces will be victorious,"[20] for example, by combining the crude pounding of the opponent into submission (use of large forces) with the finesse of a joint control hold (small forces). Although many factors contribute to the success or failure the martial artist experiences on the street or in the ring, the use of certain techniques, such as the reverse punch or the figure-four choke depending on one's style preference, might help some martial artists win fights. An un-

Proficiency in the techniques favored by your martial art, and the use of "large" and "small" forces, can increase your chances of scoring a victory, as demonstrated in this ancient artwork of a pankrationist applying a choke simultaneous to pounding his opponent into submission. *(Image source: Marie-Lan Nguyen, Wikimedia Commons)*

swerving determination also plays a crucial role. According to karate legend Mike Stone, "There are a lot of fighters I've fought who are physically stronger than I am. But I think that I have a greater desire that makes up for the difference . . . if I lack either speed, power, or ability, I try to make up for it in desire, and, you know . . . I don't want to lose . . . I have to win!"[21]

Because of the difficulties inherent in finding an ethical solution to conflict, it is not immediately apparent whether the "better" martial artist is he who relies on force to destroy the enemy's fighting capacity, or he who uses diplomacy and manages to resolve the conflict without fighting. A comment about which martial art is "better" is in place: Those who claim that traditional martial arts are not suited for the streets of modern society may be correct in the sense that a fighting art was developed to suit the terrain and counter the tactics of the particular enemy of the times. But it should also be borne in mind that the traditional martial arts were developed for the purpose of killing and not for sport or health benefits. As has been demonstrated repeatedly throughout this book, they were brutal systems of fighting that frequently resulted in the death of the losing party. Moreover, rules and safety measures imposed in competition tend to prevent modern martial artists from displaying an accurate image of an art's effectiveness.

Because of the dual nature of war where both belligerents have access to many of the same tactics, violence can generally not be avoided in one's pursuit of victory. The erroneous interpretation of Sun Tzu's emphasis on winning without bloodshed leads to the "implication that war can somehow be turned into a non-lethal intellectual exercise in which cunning and intelligence are central. On the other hand, the erroneous interpretation of Clausewitz's emphasis on force and the principle of destruction can cause force to be wielded too readily, without the careful consideration of non-military means; this would only make war more costly than necessary."[22] Despite these fallacies, when battle is inevitable both strategists considered victory the object of war. Clausewitz stated that "[v]ictory alone is not everything—but is it not, after all, what really counts?"[23]

The idea that what matters is "how one plays the game" is not advocated by either strategist and is also one of the great falsehoods of sports history. You might enjoy yourself thoroughly at a martial arts competition even if you lose, but ultimately it is winning that builds your reputation. If you do not win or win often enough, you will not progress in competition sports. An athlete who fails to win will find few opportunities to compete against more skilled opponents, and he will definitely not go to the Olympics. If competition is your game, winning is pretty much everything. If survival is your game, winning is certainly everything. When engaging an enemy, whether in actual combat or in a sanctioned bout with judges and safety personnel on standby, you must engage him with full intent on winning. If winning does not matter to you, considering the inherent dangers of combat, it is better not to fight at all.

As has been explored repeatedly, both strategists also considered a quick victory of the essence. As echoed by the ancient Greek historian Thucydides: "Consider before you enter how unexpected the chances of war be. For a long war for the most part endeth in calamity . . . And men, when they go to war, use many times to fall first to action . . . and when they have taken harm, then they fall to reasoning."[24] Although Sun Tzu and Clausewitz agreed that "a victory that is long in the coming will blunt [your] weapons and dampen [your] ardor," and a prolonged campaign will likely deplete your resources,[25] the idea that "[n]o nation has ever benefited from protracted warfare"[26] must be placed in perspective. As demonstrated in chapter 7, fighting a protracted battle from the defensive position is sometimes the wiser strategy for winning the war. However, the end goal is not to prolong battle, but to wait for a moment that will give one a relative strength advantage. Whether or not you are the instigator of battle, you can enjoy a quick victory only when your forces are superior.

Sometimes, a nation or an individual has no choice but to go to war (as may be the case if the alternative is death, rape, or injury, and even submission or humiliation), yet lacks the capacity to fight for decisive victory. A person who is kidnapped might want to rely on a protracted strategy and extend the "war" as long as possible rather than risk injury and death, in the hope that he will receive assistance from the outside. In an officially sanctioned martial arts bout, a fighter might get injured or exhaust himself prematurely and be forced to revert to fighting a protracted battle. The more difficult it is to achieve the objective, the greater the risk of long periods of inaction. Ultimately, the act of war should be a rational undertaking and lead to the achievement of some gain or higher political objective. If, as the conflict progresses, it becomes evident that you have no chance of scoring a victory, it is better to admit defeat or attempt to engage in diplomatic negotiations to save life rather than pursuing the fight. Continuing to fight simply to save face and escape humiliation at this point would be irrational.

Furthermore, numerical superiority is only one factor that increases one's relative strength advantage. A slight superiority may not guarantee victory. Sun Tzu recommended at least a two to one superiority ratio for attacking and dividing the enemy, and, if equally matched, to engage him only with some good plan.[27] Secondly, in order to benefit the most from numerical superiority, the troops

When physically inferior, a weapon can give you a strength advantage, split the opposing force, and allow you to secure the victory. (*Image source: Edith Levinet, Wikimedia Commons*)

must be brought to action at the decisive point. There are battles where the inferior force has won against greater odds, but they constitute the exception rather than the rule. Since numbers are so important, one should strive to enter the field of battle with an army as strong as possible. If the greatest number of troops one can muster proves insufficient, one must decide whether it is possible to beat the opposing force through other means such as superiority in tactics or weapons.

Although the aim for a quick and decisive victory is paramount in both Sun Tzu's and Clausewitz's opinions of combat, the nature of the aim; whether offensive (to destroy the enemy forces) or defensive (to prevent destruction), determines how one approaches battle. Combat does not happen in isolation from the surrounding circumstances. Whether combat involves a threat to your life or an agreement to accept a martial arts bout in front of a large audience, the situation tends to build over time and involves the acceptance of risk. Generally, threats away from the training hall have their roots in some kind of strategy that can be detected by an observant person before the situation has developed to the point of no return. A parallel can be drawn between Sun Tzu's focus on deception and Clausewitz's statement that "all war supposes human weakness and against that it is directed."[28] For example, a person planning to attack another is likely to lie in ambush or seek a victim that he believes is unable to counter the attack.

The ease or difficulty with which you secure the victory also has to do with the importance of the objective. If the objective is of small value (your wallet, for example), you will be less concerned with pursuing it than if it is of great value (your life or safety). Physical and mental capacities to undertake the fight determine which political objectives a person will fight for and which he will abandon. For example, a person who has rape as his goal, when discovering that his victim is no easy take, may be satisfied with merely stealing her purse. In other words, the political objective can change when he discovers that he does not have the capacity to pursue the fight in the desired manner.

Sun Tzu's *Art of War* is said to hold the key to victory, but can it prophesize how future battles should be fought? If one understands Sun Tzu's lessons, will one necessarily prevail? A war must be winnable in order to be considered a war. Otherwise we would be in a perpetual state of war and would not understand the definition of peace, in which case there could be no definition of war. Although Sun Tzu is said to have had one of the greatest military minds in history because he presented his ideas as a "cohesive, holistic philosophy of how to approach strategy,"[29] when saying that he predicted the outcome of modern wars, we are really relying on hindsight which is always clear. The idea that the *Art of War* can predict how a battle will unfold, or whether or not it is actually winnable, holds little value for future warriors or martial artists.[30]

How do you know, then, when you have achieved victory? Victory can be conceived when the enemy's loss is great in physical or moral power, or when he relinquishes his intentions. One wins wars not by conquering enemy territory, but by targeting the heart of the enemy's power. Although it has been tried many times, victory is not earned through a simple declaration. As Thucydides, the great historian of the Peloponnesian War, warned us in the fifth century BCE, first the Corinthians set up a trophy. Then the Corcyraeans, "as if they had the victory, set up a trophy likewise."[31] The Corinthians believed they were the victors, because they had caused more destruction and killed more of the enemy. The Corcyraeans, by contrast, believed they were the victors, because they had sunk thirty galleys of the Corinthians and recovered heaps of dead bodies, and because the Corinthians the previous day had rowed away from them in what was perceived as an act of cowardice.

This example illustrates why victory must be defined in order to have meaning. For example, does victory mean conquest or simply defense? Does victory mean total annihilation with significant and lasting control over a country or person's territories and political systems? Or does it merely mean winning a single battle even if you are defeated at some later date? If victory must have lasting impact, how is "lasting" defined? Winning or losing to Sun Tzu was as much a psychological as a physical state. In other words, if the defeated enemy does not acknowledge defeat, he has not lost the battle no matter how brutal the physical beating. The vanquisher must instill a mental acceptance of defeat in the vanquished. A parallel can be drawn to Daoism where the principal object is the restoration of harmony for healthy living. When one unsettles an opponent, harmony is destroyed, which leads to loss of morale. It is therefore possible to win psychologically even if the enemy forces are still intact.

As has been demonstrated repeatedly through the examples provided in this book, it is exceedingly difficult to calculate victory, or to find a formula for success that works every time. Battles are fought against a variety of opponents and under different circumstances (not all battles are fought in a 20 by 20 foot ring, for example). Not only may you have witnessed martial arts matches where you thought that one fighter was unfairly "robbed" of the decision, a martial artist who loses a match today does not have his fate determined for time and eternity, but can adjust his training methods and tactics, make a comeback tomorrow, and emerge victorious. The reverse is also true. Royce Gracie astonished the world by dominating the Ultimate Fighting Championship from 1993 to 1995. Now other fighters have moved in and taken his place in the spotlight and demonstrated that matches are won, not merely through skillfully applied chokes and arm bars, but also through the crude pounding of the opponent into submission. The focus has shifted to a methodical approach of massed attack where physical strength, endurance, and the sheer volume of blows trump cunning and finesse. This example reinforces the idea that history is seldom an accurate indicator of success or failure in future conflicts.[32]

Furthermore, whether or not your decision to fight is wise can often be evaluated only after the fight is over. If you emerged victorious, you will say that your decision was wise. If you took a beating, you will say that it was not. The fact that we have to rely on hindsight in order to determine whether or not a particular choice was sound is one reason why it is difficult to use books, including this one, to predict success or prescribe certain procedures for combat.

History does not repeat itself. Yes, we can always look back and comment that a particular person was able to use Sun Tzu's principles
successfully and score a victory. But we cannot look forward with
the same confidence and say that we will be victorious if only we
rely on the principles prescribed in his book. Since the application
of a theory of war to specific situations requires creativity and intuition, the writings of Sun Tzu should be used as pillars of strength
and not as predictions for victory.

To Clausewitz, whether or not an individual is victorious is a matter of mentality, morale, physical capacity, intellect, and practical
experience rather than theoretical reasoning or prescribed patterns
of training. One must prepare to use one's power to its fullest and
always in proportion to the enemy's resistance. If his resistance is
great, then great exertion is needed to overcome him. If certain "military virtues" such as physical strength are lacking, the combatants
must compensate for them in other ways, for example, by relying on
the defensive position until the odds can swing in one's favor.

In the end, victory is dependent on achieving the political objective. When the political objective is achieved, the aggressor will
stop fighting. A robber who asks for your wallet will take it and run
if you give it to him, because he has reached his political objective
without an exchange in blows. Although the altercation may be
resolved without bloodshed, it is the threat of combat that prompts
one to succumb to the enemy's will. Before engaging an aggressor,
one must ensure that the objective is of greater value than the sacrifice. The aggressor must likewise make a similar determination. If
the person confronting you has a weapon, you might decide that
his political object(ive), your wallet, is not worth risking your life
over, so you hand it to him. But if he threatens to kidnap you, you
might decide to fight because his political objective, possibly rape
or murder, warrants total defensive action even at the cost of injury or death.

Everything that we have studied so far—the nature and conduct
of combat, the definition of war, physical and mental preparation,
elements of tactics and strategy, imposing your will on the enemy,
the destruction of the enemy force, the strength of the defensive

Soldiers with the People's Liberation Army at Shenyang training base in China. Sometimes a display of force can prove sufficient for averting a war. *(Image source: D. Myles Cullen, Wikimedia Commons)*

position, the consequences of failure, and the value of courage and responsible action when under threat—are steppingstones toward the achievement of a lasting victory. The best way to preserve peace after victory is achieved may be by maintaining a modest attitude rather than bragging about one's feats. As reinforced by the *Ssu-ma Fu*, one of the classical Chinese military texts, "After a victory one should act as if victory had not been achieved."[33] Lasting peace can come through the total annihilation of the enemy, but it can also come through diplomacy that leads to a mutual agreement to end the conflict. How effective one is as a fighter may therefore be determined by the end and not the means; by what one achieves rather than how it is done.

The best advice that Sun Tzu and Clausewitz had for us may be that victory is prepared in the planning, and that one should not take "the first step without considering the last."[34] Or as Sun Tzu stated, "a victorious army tries to create conditions for victory before seeking battle."[35] When the goal and the steps have been identified, the manpower and weapons have been brought together, the training has been conducted, and the logistics are in place, you can fight with good spirit and be fairly confident in your ability to emerge victorious.

CONCLUSION

The objective of this book has been to give the reader the tools he or she needs to decode the ancient historical accounts of warfare in order to gain an understanding of the influence these sources have had on how we think about combat. The martial arts are often associated with Asian "ways" of fighting and self-defense. Despite the rich history and culture of Asia, they tend to be narrowly defined in the West, evoking images of *gi*-clad karateka adhering to an elusive concept called *ch'i*. As has been demonstrated throughout this book, the view that the Asian martial arts are primarily about peaceful coexistence and the avoidance of battle is historically inaccurate.

Although it has been argued that China had two major strands of military thought—the pessimistic strand which assumed that warfare was an integral part of living which made constant preparedness for war essential, and the optimistic strand which assumed that a benevolent government would prevent war—the Chinese military classics were written during a time of conflict that ended with the unification of the empire in 221 BCE.[1] Several centuries of centralized, prosperous rule followed until political fragmentation came to characterize Chinese society anew. Conscription and military campaigns against Korea became a hallmark of the early seventh century CE, resulting in impoverishment and discontent among the people and stimulating internal revolts. During the Tang Dynasty (618-907 CE), renewed efforts were made to cultivate an image of proper and benevolent rule.

Since the goal of the Chinese strategic thinkers was the preservation of a powerful and unified empire, the classic military texts focus on the relationship between the military and civilian spheres of government, social problems, and political unification.[2] Emphasis is placed on the need for reward and punishment and the use of moral force, symbolizing "the credibility of the administrative system" and the concept that winning without fighting is best.[3] The importance of studying military strategy from the lowest to the highest level is further stressed in order to avoid careless transmission of military teachings.[4] Although the texts can support many different positions through their general nature and may thus be viewed as containing weaknesses that undermine their utility, late imperial officers in China were required to study the strategic thinkers for the military service examinations.

Sun Tzu's *Art of War* is by far the best known of the ancient Chinese military classics. Although Sun Tzu's existence is debated— some historians believe that the genius behind the *Art of War* was not actually Sun Tzu, but a collection of different strategists—his legacy is not.[5] The strength of Sun Tzu's text lies in its pragmatic approach to warfare. While the Western way of war tends to present combat from the perspective of one mass army facing another at a predetermined place of battle, including an agreement that one side will claim the victory and the other will concede, warfare in Asia tended to be fought under the assumption that one army would gain an advantage through the use of deception and surprise rather than physical strength. According to Sun Tzu, warfare is not supposed to be "fair." Rules of engagement can be ignored in favor of tactics that suit the less powerful or numerically inferior army. The emergence of the Ultimate Fighting Championship and no-holds-barred contests provided an opportunity for martial artists to test the validity of Sun Tzu's theories, as evidenced through Royce Gracie's victory coming by use of good strategy and tactics rather than physical strength. A weakness of Sun Tzu's teachings is that they fail to consider the fact that neither belligerent holds a monopoly on cunning and surprise. Even if you can prevent the enemy from conquering you, there is no guarantee that you can conquer the enemy.

Like Sun Tzu, Carl von Clausewitz demonstrated that there are certain timeless elements in war. At the heart of his theory is the theme that combat is talked about in one way and exercised in another. Particularly noteworthy is his belief that success cannot be calculated according to scientific principles. Rather than providing concrete answers to questions concerning warfare, he spoke of the relationship between the many factors of war with a focus on the inherent friction of conflict. He believed that a useful theory must include all elements that pertain to battle, including morale, common sense, and logic.[6] His motivation for writing *On War* may have stemmed from a desire to gain an understanding of the dangers that faced Prussia in "a politically revolutionary and militarily resurgent France" threatening its national existence.[7] His work relies on knowledge drawn from personal experience in war and as such includes a significant amount of analysis. The "object of his work was not to provide new principles for the conduct of war, but [to provide] the essential content of what has long existed."[8] One might also note that Clausewitz's book was a work in progress when he died.

The strength of Clausewitz's text lies in the recognition that nothing in war is certain, yet he who can adapt can minimize the effects of friction. Although he stressed the importance of strength, first in general and then at the decisive point, a danger to the careless observer is that the fixation on strength can prevent one from recognizing opportunities where conflicts can be resolved through other means, such as surprise or diplomacy, and which might ultimately lead to fewer losses and less bloodshed. However, the greatest value of Clausewitz's work may lie in the recognition that "skill already developed may be refined by the study of past examples, but skill is only acquired in actually dealing with present examples, hypothetical or otherwise."[9] The martial artist can benefit from Clausewitz's teachings by first gaining an understanding of combat through extensive practice, and then using *On War* to reinforce what he already knows to be true through experience.

As has been demonstrated in this book, Sun Tzu's and Clausewitz's theories are valuable to the martial artist because they expand judgment and broaden understanding, thus bringing us a more wholesome perspective on warfare. In the end, how we use their respective theories is largely dependent on the terrain, political landscape, particular enemy one is facing, and one's personal goals in the martial arts. For example, the low and wide stances of some traditional Asian martial arts seem to inhibit mobility if used in the modern fighting arena, yet proved practical for men fighting on hilly ground that mandated good balance. As reinforced by Clausewitz, people may study the same theories or the same situations, but gain different insights, because "every age ha[s] its own kind of war, its own limiting conditions, and its own peculiar preconceptions."[10] The Japanese swordsman Miyamoto Musashi might have summed it up well when he said, "The views of each school, and the logic of each path, are realized differently according to the [mentality of the] individual person."[11]

NOTES

Introduction

1. See also Sun Wu. Tzu is an honorific title that means "master." Although Sun Tzu's work was known in the West in the eighteenth century, few good translations existed until the twentieth century. See Arthur Waldron, "Sun Tzu," *The Reader's Companion to Military History*, edited by Robert Cowley & Geoffrey Parker (New York, NY: Houghton Mifflin Company, 1996), 452.

2. See Thomas Huynh, *The Art of War: Spirituality for Conflict* (Woodstock, VT: SkyLight Path Publishing, 2008), 46.

3. This idea can be related to Carl von Clausewitz's statement that warfare should ideally be directed at the heart of the enemy with final victory the goal. See Carl von Clausewitz, *On War*, edited and translated by Michael Howard and Peter Paret (Princeton, NJ: Princeton University Press, 1976), 582. The best strategy, according to Clausewitz, is "always to be very strong; first in general, and then at the decisive point." See Hew Strachan, *Clausewitz's On War* (New York, NY: Atlantic Monthly Press, 2007), 130.

4. See G. E. Rothenberg, *Makers of Modern Strategy*, edited by Peter Paret (Princeton, NJ: Princeton University Press, 1986), 298.

5. In the 1970s, yet a book was discovered, the *Military Methods*, which appears to have been composed by Sun Pin, possibly Sun Tzu's great grandson. See Ralph D. Sawyer, *One Hundred Unorthodox Strategies: Battle and Tactics of Chinese Warfare* (Boulder, CO: Westview Press, 1996), 10.

6. See Ralph Sawyer and Mei-chün Sawyer, *The Seven Military Classics of Ancient China: including The Art of War* (Boulder, CO: Westview Press, 1993), 267.

7. Ibid., 113.

8. See Ralph Sawyer and Mei-chün Sawyer, 116. Early twentieth century Japanese karate instructor Hironori Ohtsuka noted that although violence is an element of martial arts, its purpose is to "seek and attain the way of peace and harmony." See Robert Hunt, "The Way of Harmony," *Martial Art* (Nov. 2002), 92. The idea that wars can be stopped by waging war, or by fighting fire with fire, may seem contradictory to the attainment of harmony through the balanced observance of the

yin and the yang. However, national leaders from all parts of the world have justified warfare by emphasizing that wars are fought to end all wars; in other words, out of compassion for the people.

9. See Michael Howard, *Clausewitz: A Very Short Introduction* (New York, NY: Oxford University Press, 2002), 30.

10. See John K. Fairbank, *Varieties of the Chinese Military Experience* (Cambridge, MA: Harvard University Press, 1974), 8.

11. See Ralph Sawyer and Mei-chün Sawyer, 46-47.

12. See David Graff and Robin Higham, *A Military History of China* (Boulder, CO: Westview Press, 2002), 15. While the purpose of training in the Western combat arts is to prepare for physical conflict, the Asian arts often emphasize training for the perfection of character and health. Although such views have made the classic Western texts seem less relevant to the traditional martial arts, it should be borne in mind that Chinese warfare was treated within a larger political and cultural framework. Many of the writers of Chinese military history were not practicing generals but the literate elite with ambitions extending beyond a particular campaign, which resulted in a generalized approach to writing about combat strategy and a scarcity of specific examples of battles for illustrative purposes. Sun Tzu's *Art of War* has also served as a source of inspiration in business writing. However, without understanding the underlying currents of the historical situation that served as the foundation for strategy, such exercise tends to result in misleading ideas or misguided assessment.

13. The "cookbook" approach is common in several of the ancient Chinese military texts. *Wu-Tzu*, for example, lists the eight conditions under which one engages in battle. There is also a question/answer approach in the text, where Marquis Wu asks, "If the enemy is numerous while we are few, what can I do?" and Wu Ch'i replies: "Avoid them on easy terrain, attack them in narrow quarters." See Ralph Sawyer and Mei-chün Sawyer, 220. Note that the question/answer approach can also be found in some Western texts, for example, in the dialogue between Fabrizio Colonna and Cosimo Ruccelai in Niccolo Machiavelli's *The Art of War*.

14. See Hans van de Ven, *Warfare in Chinese History* (Boston, MA: Brill Academic Publishing, 2000), 8.

15. A reason why there was a samurai class in Japan but not in China is because China relied on mobilizing large parts of the commoners against the threat coming from the steppe enemies. By contrast, the development of the samurai class in Japan prevented the commoners from carrying arms, and thus prevented individual nobility from raising large armies.

16. See Jane Hallander, "Historical Beginnings: The Evolution of the Korean Art of Kuk Sool Won," *Martial Art* (Oct. 2002), 61.
17. See Greg Brundage, "Hwarang History," *Black Belt* (Feb. 2006), 42.
18. See Jasmine Cho, "Foot Fighting," *Black Belt* (Jul. 2004), 59.
19. See Christon Archer, et al., *World History of Warfare* (Lincoln, NE: University of Nebraska Press, 2002), 79.
20. Ibid., 140. Note that the Middle Age, or medieval period, is mostly a Western concept.
21. See Peter Paret, *Makers of Modern Strategy*, edited by Peter Paret (Princeton, NJ: Princeton University Press, 1986), 187.
22. See Howard, 32.
23. Although Clausewitz avoided the "cookbook" approach, remarkable similarities to the Asian texts can be found in other Western works. For example, Antoine-Henri Jomini, who wrote about the Napoleonic wars, listed "six distinct parts" to the art of war, and "twelve essential conditions" for making a perfect army. See A. H. Jomini, *The Art of War*, translated by H. Mendell and W. P. Craighill (Philadelphia, PA: Lippincott, 1879), Article XIII.
24. See Carl von Clausewitz, *On War*, edited by Anatol Rapoport (New York, NY: Penguin Classics, 1982), 22.
25. See Strachan, 56.
26. The media has fueled popular interest in the subject for several decades through releases of such movies and television shows as Karate Kid, Blood Sport, and Walker, Texas Ranger; through televised sports events such as the Ultimate Fighting Championship; and through documentary series such as the Human Weapon.
27. See John A. Lynn, *Battle: A History of Combat and Culture* (Cambridge, MA: Westview Press, 2003), 44.

Chapter 1

1. See Gregory E. LeBlanc, "Sticky Hands: The Fighting Soul of Wing Chun Lives On in Chi Sao Training," *Black Belt* (Sep. 2003), 95.
2. Jonathan Maberry, "Myths and Misconceptions," *Black Belt* (Jan. 2006), 97.
3. See Clausewitz, *On War*, edited and translated by Michael Howard and Peter Paret, 127.
4. Bujutsu, the military fighting arts of Japan, differ from budo (military way) by focusing on combat to the death rather than on personal achievement and self-improvement. See Jose Fraguas, "Lost Along the Way," interview with William J. Dometrich, *Martial Art* (Jul. 2003), 84-85.

5. See Ralph D. Sawyer, 6.
6. See Kathleen Ryor, *Military Culture in Imperial China*, edited by Nicola Di Cosmo (Cambridge, MA: Harvard University Press, 2009), 223.
7. See Joanna Waley-Cohen, *Military Culture in Imperial China*, edited by Nicola Di Cosmo (Cambridge, MA: Harvard University Press, 2009), 281 & 292.
8. See Ralph D. Sawyer, 68.
9. See Walther Heissig, "Tracing Some Mongol Oral Motifs in a Chinese Prosimetric Ming Novel of 1478," *Asian Folklore Studies*, Vol. 53, No. 2 (1994), 231-243
10. See Ralph Sawyer and Mei-chün Sawyer, 53.
11. See Art of War, Sun Tzu Documentary, History Channel (Jul. 13, 2009). Note that diplomacy does not have as much relevance in sports competition as it does in real-life events. If two martial arts competitors refuse to engage in combat and instead settle the match "peacefully," the audience will no doubt be disappointed.
12. See Subrata Saha, *China's Grand Strategy: From Confucius to Contemporary*, U.S. Army War College.
13. See Nicola Di Cosmo, *Military Culture in Imperial China*, edited by Nicola Di Cosmo (Cambridge, MA: Harvard University Press, 2009), 18.
14. See Blue Johnson, "Shorinji Kempo: This Little-Known Offspring of Shaolin Kung Fu is Alive and Kicking in Japan—and Making Inroads in the USA!" *Black Belt* (Sep. 2002), 57.
15. See Michael Rosenbaum, *Kata and the Transmission of Knowledge in Traditional Martial Arts* (Boston, MA: YMAA Publication Center, 2004), 42.
16. See Terry L. Wilson, "Shock & Awe," *Martial Art* (Sep. 2003), 57
17. Yamamoto Tsunetomo, *Hagakure: The Book of the Samurai*, Chapter 7. The same principle held true for the Western soldier fighting on modern battlefields hundreds of years later, as evidenced by soldier notes from the late nineteenth century. The similarity is striking: If his bayonet broke, the soldier would strike with the stock; if the stock gave way, he would hit with his fists; if his fists were hurt, he would bite with his teeth. See Christopher Amberger, "Classifications of Combat," *Blackfriar's Journal*, from M. I. Dragomiroff's *Notes for Soldiers*, c. 1890.
18. Miyamoto Musashi, *A Book of Five Rings*, translated by Victor Harris (Woodstock, NY: The Overlook Press, 1974), 86-87.
19. See Dan Ivan, "Defense Against a Punch," *Martial Arts & Combat Sports* (Aug. 2002), 51.
20. See Jose Fraguas, "Forever Budo," interview with Fumio Demura, *Martial Art* (Sep. 2003), 29.

21. See Mark Cheng, "Hard School of the Soft Art," *Black Belt* (May 2004), 114.

22. See Stephen Petermann with Loren Franck, "Shatter Your Nightmares," *Martial Art* (Aug. 2003), 53-54.

23. See Massad Ayoob, "Greek Pankration: The Ancient Art of All-Power Combat," *Black Belt* (Oct. 2005), 94.

24. See Frank Daros, "Greek Pankration," interview with Jim Arvanitis, *Black Belt* (Sep. 2004), 100-105. The martial arts were written about and studied by the elite or commoners, depending on the military establishment's relation to the state. States have at times chosen to employ mainly the nobility in the armed forces, and at other times mainly commoners and mercenaries.

25. See Ayoob, 96.

26. See Tao Hanzhang, *Sun Tzu's Art of War: The Modern Chinese Interpretation*, translated by Yuan Shibing (New York, NY: Sterling Innovation, 2006), 52.

27. See Michael I. Handel, *Masters of War: Classical Strategic Thought* (New York, NY: Routledge, 2001), xv.

28. Sun Tzu, *The Art of War*, translated by Thomas Cleary (Boston, MA: Shambhala Publications, 1988), 95.

29. See Gabriel Suarez, "Musashi for the 21st Century," *Black Belt* (May 2004), 66.

30. See Jason K. Martin, "Code of Isshin-Ryu: Karate's Deepest Meaning Can Be Extracted from a Handful of Cryptic Statements," *Black Belt* (Sep. 2002), 73.

31. See Jose Fraguas, "The Snow Tiger Roars," interview with Bong Soo Han, *Martial Art* (Jul. 2003), 34.

32. Zhang Yun, *The Art of Chinese Swordsmanship* (Boston, MA: Weatherhill, 1998), 265.

33. See Thomas J. Nardi, "Folklore of Tai Chi," *Martial Art* (Jul. 2003), 53.

34. See Ralph Sawyer and Mei-chün Sawyer, 180.

35. Ibid., 327.

36. See Howard, 41.

37. Sun Tzu, *The Art of War*, translated by Lionel Giles (New York, NY: Barnes and Nobles Classics, 2003), 16.

38. Clausewitz, *On War*, edited and translated by Michael Howard and Peter Paret, 195.

39. Ibid., 3.

40. Niccolo Machiavelli, *The Historical, Political, and Diplomatic Writings of Niccolo Machiavelli, Vol. 2*, translated by Christian E. Detmold (Boston, MA: James R. Osgood and Company, 1882), 422.

41. See W. Hock Hochheim, "12 Combat Commandments from the School of Hard Knocks," *Black Belt* (Aug. 2003), 60.
42. See Jason William McNeil, "Slammin' Shuai Chiao," *Black Belt* (Jul. 2004), 100.
43. See Cho, 59.
44. Tamas Weber, "Budo on the Battlefield," interview by Jose Fraguas, *Martial Arts & Combat Sports* (Jun. 2002), 61.
45. Thucydides, *The Peloponnesian War* (New York, NY: E. P. Dutton, 1910), Section 1.71.

Chapter 2

1. See Ralph D. Sawyer, 34.
2. See Dave Lowry, "What's in a Name?" *Black Belt* (Jan. 2006), 44-46.
3. Yamamoto Tsunetomo, *Hagakure: The Book of the Samurai*, translated by William Scott Wilson (New York, NY: Kodansha, 1983).
4. Many of Carl von Clausewitz's thoughts on warfare are remarkably similar to Sun Tzu's. However, although Sun Tzu's *Art of War* was translated approximately two hundred years ago, and "was reportedly studied and effectively employed by Napoleon," it is unlikely that Clausewitz had studied Sun Tzu, and more likely that he came to his conclusions after many years of personal experience of war. See Ralph Sawyer and Mei-chün Sawyer, 149.
5. Jim Wagner, "The Fast-Food Menu Concept," *Black Belt* (Aug. 2005), 48. Proponents of modern Western martial arts, such as krav maga, claim that these arts are continuously enhanced to meet the demands of fighting in the contemporary world. As more information about the enemy emerges, new techniques are integrated as seen fit.
6. See Tao Hanzhang, 22.
7. Ibid., 44.
8. See Miyamoto Musashi, *The Book of Five Rings*, translated by Thomas Cleary (Boston, MA: Shambhala, 2005), 9.
9. See Hew Strachan and Andreas Herberg-Rothe, editors, *Clausewitz in the Twenty-First Century* (New York, NY: Oxford University Press, 2007), 197
10. Gichin Funakoshi, *Karate-Do Kyohan: The Master Text* (New York: NY: Kodansha America, Inc., 1973), 238.
11. Since taking the initiative by setting the time and place for battle is not always possible, many of Sun Tzu's statements should be used as guiding principles rather than adhered to blindly. His advocacy of winning without fighting, or through deception by exploiting the ad-

versary's strength, is perhaps more relevant in a street confrontation, for example, if one has the option of offering some calming words or walking away without physically engaging the adversary.

12. Clausewitz acknowledged that some confrontations can be resolved without resorting to physical force, for example, by diplomatic means that lead to a mutual agreement to avoid engagement. The difference between Sun Tzu's and Clausewitz's views is that Clausewitz would not have defined diplomatic action as an element of war. Furthermore, he who desires to use physical intimidation as a deterrence in the hope that a fight will not take place, must still be fully prepared to engage in battle, to fight and shed blood if need be.

13. See Strachan, 14 & 137. Clausewitz's military theory was also evident in his personality. When he "was put forward as a possible ambassador to London in 1821 . . . he was deemed to be too brusque, too undiplomatic, and—above all—too radical for such a post." See Strachan, 64.

14. United States Marine Corps, *Warfighting*, 1989, based on Clausewitz's *On War*, 32-33.

15. Not synonymous with intelligence in the traditional sense, judgment depends on natural talent rather than on classroom learning; it is capability and decisiveness.

16. See Tao Hanzhang, 45.

17. See Huynh, 148. A prescriptive theory of war prescribes the means by which one achieves success. A descriptive theory of war analyzes combat without suggesting a solution to a particular problem. A descriptive theory can lead to a prescriptive theory after sufficient analysis has been conducted to determine which elements can be used with greater efficiency than others.

18. See Handel, 41.

19. See Jon Tetsuro Sumida, *Decoding Clausewitz: A New Approach to On War* (Lawrence, KS: University Press of Kansas, 2008), 54.

20. Clausewitz, *On War*, edited by Anatol Rapoport, 223.

21. See Robert H. Larson, "Max Jähns and the Writing of Military History in Imperial Germany," *The Journal of Military History*, Vol. 72, No. 2 (Apr. 2008), 354.

22. Keith Vargo, "Way of the Warrior: Martial Art or Martial Science," *Black Belt* (Feb. 2003), 28.

23. See Strachan, 74.

24. See Tao Hanzhang, 34.

25. See Huynh, 60-61.

26. See Tao Hanzhang, 39.

27. See John Corcoran and Emil Farkas with Stuart Sobel, *The Original Martial Arts Encyclopedia: Tradition and History* (Los Angeles, CA: Pro-Action Publishing, 1993), 18.
28. Ibid., 105-110.
29. See Tao Hanzhang, 76.
30. See Handel, 44.

Chapter 3

1. See Doug Jeffrey, "Strict Eyes: Shotokan Great Tsutomu Ohshima Opens Up During a Rare Interview," *Martial Art* (Aug. 2003), 36.
2. See Ralph Sawyer and Mei-chün Sawyer, 155-156.
3. See Waley-Cohen, 283.
4. See Ralph D. Sawyer, 42.
5. See Allen Fung, "Testing the Self-Strengthening: The Chinese Army in the Sino-Japanese War of 1894-1895," *Modern Asian Studies*, Vol. 30, No. 4, Special Issue: War in Modern China (Oct. 1996), 1024-1026.
6. See Ralph Sawyer and Mei-chün Sawyer, 151-153.
7. See Tao Hanzhang, 57.
8. See Ralph Sawyer and Mei-chün Sawyer, 113.
9. See Tao Hanzhang, 23.
10. Ibid., 46.
11. Zhuge Liang, *The Way of the General*, translated by Thomas Cleary, http://kongming.net/novel/writings/wotg/.
12. See Rev. Kensho Furuya, "Internal Power: How to Cultivate Ki in Aikido," *Martial Art* (Nov. 2002), 39.
13. See Hirokazu Kanazawa, "Purely Traditional: The Teaching and Philosophy of Hirokazu Kanazawa," interview by Jose Fraguas, *Martial Art* (Oct. 2002), 31.
14. See Petermann, 54.
15. See Keith Vargo, "Way of the Warrior: Truth Seekers," *Black Belt* (May 2004), 24.
16. See Ralph Sawyer and Mei-chün Sawyer, 242.
17. See Tao Hanzhang, 94.
18. See Brian Jacobs, "Birth of Judo," *Black Belt* (Sep. 2004), 94 & 96. Traditional martial arts sometimes encompass healing practices. Knowledge of how to resuscitate a person who has been harmed in combat gives the student the ability to choose whether to kill or heal, and can be a tremendous source of power. See Jacobs, 93-94.
19. See Ralph Sawyer and Mei-chün Sawyer, 69.
20. See PBS, *Secrets of the Samurai Sword: Way of the Warrior*, Nova, http://www.pbs.org/wgbh/nova/samurai/way-nf.html.

21. Mark Cheng, "Legends of Kung Fu: The Arts Are Still Evolving," *Black Belt* (Sep. 2002), 24.

22. See Corcoran and Farkas, 88.

23. Ibid., 90-91. During the Wei and Qi dynasties approximately 1,500 years ago, Chinese emperor Xiaowen built a monastery deep in the woods at the foot of the Shaoshi Mountain, and named it Shao-lin (lin refers to woods).

24. For more information about the Shaolin monks and their rigorous kung-fu regimen, please refer to the excellent documentaries found on the National Geographic Channel.

25. See Xue Fei, "Know Your Major: Sanda," *Global Times* (Dec. 29, 2009).

26. See Howard, 29.

27. Clausewitz, *On War*, edited and translated by Michael Howard and Peter Paret, 101.

28. Lt. Col. Dave Grossman with Loren Christensen, *On Combat: The Psychology and Physiology of Deadly Conflict in War and in Peace* (Belleville, IL: PPCT Research Publications, 2004), 197.

29. Ibid., 36.

30. John Keegan, *The Face of Battle* (New York, NY: Penguin Books, 1976), 18.

31. Clausewitz, *On War*, edited and translated by Michael Howard and Peter Paret, 6.

32. See Strachan, 125.

33. B. H. Liddell Hart, *The Classic Book on Military Strategy* (London, England: Faber & Faber, 1954), 3.

Chapter 4

1. Sun Tzu, *The Art of War*, translated by Thomas Cleary, 166.

2. See Tao Hanzhang, 24.

3. See Ralph D. Sawyer, 81.

4. See Tao Hanzhang, 80.

5. Clausewitz, *On War*, edited by Anatol Rapoport, 252.

6. See Dan Ivan, "Sizzling Stances," *Martial Art* (Aug. 2003), 59-63.

7. See Ralph D. Sawyer, 23.

8. See John Clements, *Medieval Swordsmanship: Illustrated Methods and Techniques* (Boulder, CO: Paladin Press, 1998), 121.

9. See Tao Hanzhang, 73-74.

10. Ibid., 128.

11. Ibid., 84.

12. Ibid., 35.
13. Chris Crudelli, *The Way of the Warrior: Martial Arts and Fighting Styles from Around the World* (London, England: DK Adult, 2008), 125.
14. See Tao Hanzhang, 45.
15. See J. Torres, "Continuous Fist Fighting," interview with Sid Campbell, *Black Belt* (May 2004), 100-102 & 126.
16. See United States Marine Corps, *Warfighting*, 1989, based on Clausewitz's *On War*, 36. Although the Western military tradition emphasizes direct attack and pitting strength against strength, the purpose of movement is ultimately to gain a strategic advantage that allows one to exploit the enemy's numerical superiority, for example, by attacking his flanks. Or, as Sun Tzu said, appear weak when you are strong and strong when you are weak. Attacking the enemy's weak points by luring him into a position of inferiority allows one to retain the initiative.
17. See Huynh, 119.
18. See Tao Hanzhang, 24.
19. See Handel, 218.
20. See Huynh, 75.
21. See Tao Hanzhang, 50.
22. Although drawn from the field of physics, center of gravity is a metaphor used to illustrate a concept. It is not intended to imply that Clausewitz relied on physics as a science for his war strategies.
23. Clausewitz, *On War*, edited and translated by Michael Howard and Peter Paret, 198.
24. See Clausewitz, *On War*, edited by Anatol Rapoport, 270-271.
25. See Strachan, 112.

Chapter 5

1. See Tao Hanzhang, 49.
2. See Strachan, 142.
3. Although nonresistance is commonly thought of as less brutal than aggressive offense, perhaps because of Daoist thinking which purpose it is to neutralize the fight so that harmony can be restored, it is an effective option that allows the martial artist to seize the initiative with minimum energy expenditure.
4. See William C. C. Hu and Kim Pyung Soo, "Korean Ssirum Wrestling," *Black Belt* (Sep. 2004), 70-73.
5. See George Alexander, "Shaolin Ancestors," *Martial Art* (Aug. 2003), 40.
6. See Patrick McCarthy, *Bubishi: The Bible of Karate* (Boston, MA: Tuttle Publishing, 1995), 27.

7. See Dennis Rovere, *The Xingyi Quan of the Chinese Army*, translated by Chow Hon Huen (Berkeley, California: Blue Snake Books, 2008), xviii-xix.
8. See Martin, 73.
9. See Handel, 166.
10. Ibid., 171.
11. See Lucas Wiltse, "Good Kung Fu: Meeting Wing Chun Master Lo Man Kam," *Travel in Taiwan* (Jul. / Aug. 2010), 49.
12. See Corcoran and Farkas, 137.
13. See Tony Wolf, "A System Which He Termed Bartitsu," *Journal of Manly Arts: European and Colonial Combatives, 1776-1914* (May 2006).
14. See The History Channel, *Human Weapon*, for more detailed information about the history, training, and combat applications of Russian sambo.
15. See Rovere, 7.

Chapter 6

1. See Huynh, 59.
2. See Handel, 166.
3. See Huynh, 113.
4. See Handel, 54.
5. Clausewitz, *On War*, edited by Anatol Rapoport, 276.
6. See Handel, 157.
7. Clausewitz, *On War*, edited by Anatol Rapoport, 345.
8. See Tao Hanzhang 34. Sun Tzu was quite precise in his calculation of strength: "When ten to the enemy's one, surround him. When five times his strength, attack him. If double his strength, divide him. If equally matched, you may engage him with some good plan." See Hanzhang, 34.
9. Ibid., 70.
10. Ibid., 49.
11. Clausewitz, *On War*, edited by Anatol Rapoport, 265.
12. See Strachan, 163.
13. See Corcoran and Farkas, 74.
14. Clausewitz, *On War*, edited by Anatol Rapoport, 306.
15. See Wally Jay, *Small-Circle Jujitsu* (Valencia, CA: Ohara Publications, 1989), 25.
16. See Bruce Tegner, *Savate: French Foot & Fist Fighting* (Ventura, CA: Thor Publishing Company, 1983), 14.
17. Please refer to the National Geographic Channel, *Human Weapon* for more information about savate.

18. See Handel, 279.
19. Ibid., 140. Sun Tzu, by contrast, argued that if possible, one should try to make peace without destroying the enemy forces by making them move over to one's side. It is possible, I suppose, to make a friend of a former enemy in the martial arts. However, much of the training takes place under the assumption that battle will have to be fought. Needless to say, there could be no martial arts competition if the two "belligerents" decided to "make peace" and become friends before entering the ring.
20. See Ralph Sawyer and Mei-chün Sawyer, 121.

Chapter 7

1. See David Graff and Robin Higham, 13.
2. See Ralph Sawyer and Mei-chün Sawyer, 353.
3. See Huynh, 49.
4. See Strachan, 157.
5. Carl von Clausewitz may have considered defense the stronger form of war because of the Napoleonic Wars and Prussia's political situation at the time. See Tetsuro Sumida, 79.
6. See Ralph D. Sawyer, 112.
7. See Ralph Sawyer and Mei-chün Sawyer, 346-348.
8. See James W. McNeil, "Splashing Hands: A Splash of Kung-Fu," *Inside Kung-Fu*, http://insidekung-fu.com/.
9. See Strachan, 94.
10. See Ralph Sawyer and Mei-chün Sawyer, 160.
11. See Blue Johnson, "Never Attack First," *Martial Art* (Jul. 2003), 37-40 & 95.
12. See Jose Fraguas, "The Snow Tiger Roars," 35.
13. Similarly, the Cold War between the United States and the Soviet Union would not have been classified as a war per Clausewitz.
14. Clausewitz, *On War*, edited and translated by Michael Howard and Peter Paret, 357.
15 . See Ralph Sawyer and Mei-chün Sawyer, 90.

Chapter 8

1. See Handel, 276.
2. See Ralph Sawyer and Mei-chün Sawyer, 177.
3. See Sid Campbell, *Kobudo and Bugei: The Ancient Weapon Way of Okinawa and Japan* (Boulder, CO: Paladin Press, 1998), 1.

4. See Andrew Scobell, *China's Use of Military Force: Beyond the Great Wall and the Long March* (New York, NY: Cambridge University Press, 2003), 34.
5. See Miyamoto Musahsi, *A Book of Five Rings*, translated by Victor Harris, 74.
6. Ibid., 61.
7. Ibid., 56.
8. See Corcoran and Farkas, 92.
9. See Ralph Sawyer and Mei-chün Sawyer, 120.

Chapter 9

1. See Huynh, 66.
2. Clausewitz, *On War*, edited by Anatol Rapoport, 140.
3. Ibid., 139.
4. Ibid., 140.
5. See Richard Cohen, *By the Sword: A History of Gladiators, Musketeers, Samurai, Swashbucklers, and Olympic Champions* (New York, NY: Modern Library, 2002), 41.
6. See Archer, et al., 79.
7. Clausewitz, *On War*, edited by Anatol Rapoport, 142.
8. See Tao Hanzhang, 30.
9. Ibid., 34.
10. Ibid., 85.
11. Ibid., 63.
12. Ibid., 90.
13. Clausewitz, *On War*, edited by Anatol Rapoport, 260.
14. See Huynh, 91.
15. See Armstrong Starkey, "Paoli to Stony Point: Military Ethics and Weaponry during the American Revolution," *The Journal of Military History*, Vol. 58, No. 1 (Jan. 1994), 27.
16. Kyung Won Chung, "Guest Editorial," *Black Belt* (Apr. 2003), 12.
17. See Ralph D. Sawyer, 83.
18. Victor Davis Hanson, *The Father of Us All: War and History* (New York, NY: Bloomsbury Press, 2010), 48.
19. See Miyamoto Musashi, *A Book of Five Rings*, translated by Victor Harris, 45.
20. Clausewitz, *On War*, edited by Anatol Rapoport, 259.
21. Ibid., 259.
22. One reason why fine motor skill joint control techniques prove effective for police officers who must be ready to handle the chaos of the streets at a moment's notice, is because the police officer holds the

initiative from the start; he does not attempt to apply the joint lock in the midst of an ambush. By the time he applies the lock, the suspect has already been subdued by other means.

23. See David Rogers, "No-Nonsense Kung-Fu," *Inside Kung-Fu*, http://www.insidekung-fu.com.

24. Clausewitz, *On War*, edited by Anatol Rapoport, 160.

25. See Tao Hanzhang, 45.

26. See Corcoran and Farkas, 5.

27. Thucydides, *The Peloponnesian War: The Complete Hobbes Translation*, with notes and introduction by David Grene (Chicago, IL: University of Chicago Press, 1989), 67-68.

28. See Tao Hanzhang, 80.

29. See Handel, 276.

30. See Tao Hanzhang, 81.

31. See Chrissy Koeth, "An Open Mind: Once You Open the Mind, a World of Infinite Possibilities Exists," *Inside Kung-Fu*, http://www.insidekung-fu.com/.

32. See Handel, 84.

Chapter 10

1. See Colin S. Gray, *Defining and Achieving Decisive Victory*, Strategic Studies Institute (Apr. 2002), 21.

2. See Martin van Creveld, "War," *The Reader's Companion to Military History*, edited by Robert Cowley & Geoffrey Parker (New York, NY: Houghton Mifflin Company, 1996), 499.

3. See Ralph Sawyer and Mei-chün Sawyer, 247.

4. See Clausewitz, *On War*, edited by Anatol Rapoport, 161-162.

5. See Tao Hanzhang, 40.

6. See Handel, 113.

7. Saha.

8. See Handel, 147.

9. Ibid., 157.

10. See Sun Tzu, *The Art of War*, translated by Thomas Cleary, 166.

11. See Ralph D. Sawyer, 213.

12. Victor Davis Hanson, *Ripples of Battle* (New York, NY: Anchor Books, 2003), 59.

13. See Huynh, 184-185.

14. Saha.

15. Clausewitz, *On War*, edited by Anatol Rapoport, 218.

16. See Handel, xxi.

17. Clausewitz, *On War*, edited by Anatol Rapoport, 330.

18. Ibid., 424.

19. The reason why Napoleon Bonaparte was so admired, even to this day, was not because he was a particularly ethical strategist nor because he had any kind of inherent right to fight for territory, but because he was successful. The same applies to Alexander the Great.

20. See Huynh, 41.

21. See Al Weiss and David Weiss, *The Official History of Karate in America: The Golden Age: 1968-1986* (Los Angeles, CA: Pro-Action Publishing, 1997), 40.

22. Handel, 153.

23. Ibid., 315.

24. Thucydides, *The Peloponnesian War: The Complete Hobbes Translation*, 46.

25. See Ralph Sawyer and Mei-chün Sawyer, 159.

26. See Huynh, 21.

27. See Tao Hanzhang, 34.

28. Clausewitz, *On War*, edited and translated by Michael Howard and Peter Paret, 341.

29. See Art of War, Sun Tzu Documentary.

30. While it is tempting to use historical examples as guidelines for future strategy, one must remember that the soldiers on the battlefield lack the benefit of hindsight. The lessons must thus be placed in context and viewed as pillars of strength, not as equations for victory. Harry S. Truman's often quoted statement, *"It is amazing what you can accomplish, if you do not care who gets the credit,"* offers a good example. What were the times and circumstances when Truman uttered those words? What were the personalities of the people involved? What were their backgrounds, goals, and desires? How can you remove an idea from a time sixty years in the past, and with the quick lash of your tongue transport it to the immediacy of today, and place it in a different group of people under a different set of circumstances; in short, in a different world, and think that nothing has changed? Although Truman's presidency influenced a variety of war plans and foreign affairs, if we search history for examples of how war (or peace) should be conducted, we are likely to find numerous models that support whichever view we wish to take.

31. Thucydides, *The Peloponnesian War: The Complete Hobbes Translation*, 32.

32. History can seldom be used to determine how or when a future conflict will begin or end. The author challenges the reader to examine the truth or fallibility of the saying that "history repeats itself."

33. See Ralph D. Sawyer, 155.

34. Clausewitz, *On War*, edited by Michael Howard and Peter Paret, 584.

35. See Tao Hanzhang, 200.

Conclusion

1. From Ken Swope, *Continuing Strategic Traditions & Creating Strategic Cultures*, Lecture (Norwich University, VT, 2006).

2. See Christopher C. Rand, "Li Ch'uan and Chinese Military Thought," *Harvard Journal of Asian Studies*, Vol. 39, No. 1 (Jun. 1979), 107-108.

3. See Ralph Sawyer and Mei-chün Sawyer, 197.

4. Ibid., 360.

5. See Art of War, Sun Tzu Documentary.

6. See Clausewitz, *On War*, edited and translated by Michael Howard and Peter Paret, 190.

7. See Tetsuro Sumida, xvi.

8. Strachan, 79.

9. Dallas D. Irvine, "The French Discovery of Clausewitz and Napoleon," *The Journal of the American Military Institute*, Vol. 4, No. 3 (Autumn 1940), 144.

10. Clausewitz, *On War*, edited and translated by Michael Howard and Peter Paret, 593.

11. Miyamoto Musashi, *Book of Five Rings*, translated by Thomas Cleary, 58.

BIBLIOGRAPHY

Alexander, George. "Shaolin Ancestors." *Martial Art* (Aug. 2003).

Amberger, Christopher. "Classifications of Combat." *Blackfriar's Journal.* From M. I. Dragomiroff's *Notes for Soldiers,* c. 1890.

Archer, Christon, et al. *World History of Warfare.* Lincoln, NE: University of Nebraska Press, 2002.

Art of War. Sun Tzu Documentary. History Channel (Jul. 13, 2009).

Ayoob, Massad. "Greek Pankration: The Ancient Art of All-Power Combat." *Black Belt* (Oct. 2005).

Brundage, Greg. "Hwarang History." *Black Belt* (Feb. 2006).

Campbell, Sid. *Kobudo and Bugei: The Ancient Weapon Way of Okinawa and Japan.* Boulder, CO: Paladin Press, 1998.

Cheng, Mark. "Hard School of the Soft Art." *Black Belt* (May 2004).

.........."Legends of Kung Fu: The Arts Are Still Evolving." *Black Belt* (Sep. 2002).

Cho, Jasmine. "Foot Fighting." *Black Belt* (Jul. 2004).

Clausewitz, Carl von. *On War.* Edited and translated by Michael Howard and Peter Paret. Princeton, NJ: Princeton University Press, 1976.

..........*On War.* Edited by Anatol Rapoport. New York, NY: Penguin Classics, 1982.

Clements, John. *Medieval Swordsmanship: Illustrated Methods and Techniques.* Boulder, CO: Paladin Press, 1998.

Cohen, Richard. *By the Sword: A History of Gladiators, Musketeers, Samurai, Swashbucklers, and Olympic Champions.* New York, NY: Modern Library, 2002.

Corcoran, John and Farkas, Emil with Sobel, Stuart. *The Original Martial Arts Encyclopedia: Tradition and History.* Los Angeles, CA: Pro-Action Publishing, 1993.

Creveld, Martin van. "War," The Reader's Companion to Military History. Edited by Robert Cowley & Geoffrey Parker. New York, NY: Houghton Mifflin Company, 1996.

Crudelli, Chris. The Way of the Warrior: Martial Arts and Fighting Styles from Around the World. London, England: DK Adult, 2008.

Daros, Frank. "Greek Pankration." Interview with Jim Arvanitis. Black Belt (Sep. 2004).

Di Cosmo, Nicola. Military Culture in Imperial China. Edited by Nicola Di Cosmo. Cambridge, MA: Harvard University Press, 2009.

Fairbank, John K. Varieties of the Chinese Military Experience. Cambridge, MA: Harvard University Press, 1974.

Fraguas, Jose. "Forever Budo." Interview with Fumio Demura. Martial Art (Sep. 2003).

.........."Lost Along the Way." Interview with William J. Dometrich. Martial Art (Jul. 2003).

.........."The Snow Tiger Roars." Interview with Bong Soo Han. Martial Art (Jul. 2003).

Fung, Allen. "Testing the Self-Strengthening: The Chinese Army in the Sino-Japanese War of 1894-1895." Modern Asian Studies, Vol. 30, No. 4, Special Issue: War in Modern China (Oct. 1996).

Gichin Funakoshi. Karate-Do Kyohan: The Master Text. New York: NY: Kodansha America, Inc., 1973.

Graff, David and Higham, Robin. A Military History of China. Boulder, CO: Westview Press, 2002.

Gray, Colin S. Defining and Achieving Decisive Victory. Strategic Studies Institute (Apr. 2002).

Grossman, Dave, Lt. Col. with Christensen, Loren. On Combat: The Psychology and Physiology of Deadly Conflict in War and in Peace. Belleville, IL: PPCT Research Publications, 2004.

Hallander, Jane. "Historical Beginnings: The Evolution of the Korean Art of Kuk Sool Won." Martial Art (Oct. 2002).

Handel, Michael I. Masters of War: Classical Strategic Thought. New York, NY: Routledge, 2001.

Hanson, Victor Davis. Ripples of Battle. New York, NY: Anchor Books, 2003.

.........The Father of Us All: War and History. New York, NY: Bloomsbury Press, 2010.

Heissig, Walther. "Tracing Some Mongol Oral Motifs in a Chinese Prosimetric Ming Novel of 1478." Asian Folklore Studies, Vol. 53, No. 2 (1994).

Hirokazu Kanazawa. "Purely Traditional: The Teaching and Philosophy of Hirokazu Kanazawa." Interview by Jose Fraguas. Martial Art (Oct. 2002).

Hochheim, W. Hock. "12 Combat Commandments from the School of Hard Knocks." Black Belt (Aug. 2003).

Howard, Michael. Clausewitz: A Very Short Introduction. New York, NY: Oxford University Press, 2002.

Hu, William C. C. and Pyung Soo, Kim. "Korean Ssirum Wrestling." Black Belt (Sep. 2004).

Hunt, Robert. "The Way of Harmony." Martial Art (Nov. 2002).

Huynh, Thomas. The Art of War: Spirituality for Conflict. Woodstock, VT: SkyLight Path Publishing, 2008.

Irvine, Dallas D. "The French Discovery of Clausewitz and Napoleon." The Journal of the American Military Institute, Vol. 4, No. 3 (Autumn 1940).

Ivan, Dan. "Defense Against a Punch." Martial Arts & Combat Sports (Aug. 2002).

.........."Sizzling Stances." Martial Art (Aug. 2003).

Jacobs, Brian. "Birth of Judo." Black Belt (Sep. 2004).

Jay, Wally. Small-Circle Jujitsu. Valencia, CA: Ohara Publications, 1989.

Jeffrey, Doug. "Strict Eyes: Shotokan Great Tsutomu Ohshima Opens Up During a Rare Interview." Martial Art (Aug. 2003).

Johnson, Blue. "Never Attack First." Martial Art (Jul. 2003).

.........."Shorinji Kempo: This Little-Known Offspring of Shaolin Kung Fu is Alive and Kicking in Japan—and Making Inroads in the USA!" Black Belt (Sep. 2002).

Jomini, A. H. The Art of War. Translated by H. Mendell and W. P. Craighill. Philadelphia, PA: Lippincott, 1879.

Keegan, John. The Face of Battle. New York, NY: Penguin Books, 1976.

Kensho Furuya, Rev. "Internal Power: How to Cultivate Ki in Aikido." Martial Art (Nov. 2002).

Koeth, Chrissy. "An Open Mind: Once You Open the Mind, a World of Infinite Possibilities Exists." Inside Kung-Fu. http://www.insidekung-fu.com/.

Kyung Won Chung. "Guest Editorial." Black Belt (Apr. 2003).

Larson, Robert H. "Max Jähns and the Writing of Military History in Imperial Germany." The Journal of Military History, Vol. 72, No. 2 (Apr. 2008).

LeBlanc, Gregory E. "Sticky Hands: The Fighting Soul of Wing Chun Lives On in Chi Sao Training." Black Belt (Sep. 2003).

Liddell Hart, B. H. The Classic Book on Military Strategy. London, England: Faber & Faber, 1954.

Lowry, Dave. "What's in a Name?" Black Belt (Jan. 2006).

Lynn, John A. Battle: A History of Combat and Culture. Cambridge, MA: Westview Press, 2003.

Maberry, Jonathan. "Myths and Misconceptions." Black Belt (Jan. 2006).

Machiavelli, Niccolo. The Historical, Political, and Diplomatic Writings of Niccolo Machiavelli, Vol. 2. Translated by Christian E. Detmold. Boston, MA: James R. Osgood and Company, 1882.

Martin, Jason K. "Code of Isshin-Ryu: Karate's Deepest Meaning Can Be Extracted from a Handful of Cryptic Statements." Black Belt (Sep. 2002).

McCarthy, Patrick. Bubishi: The Bible of Karate. Boston, MA: Tuttle Publishing, 1995.

McNeil, James. "Splashing Hands: A Splash of Kung-Fu." Inside Kung-Fu. http://insidekung-fu.com/.

McNeil, Jason William. "Slammin' Shuai Chiao." Black Belt (Jul. 2004).

Miyamoto Musashi. A Book of Five Rings. Translated by Victor Harris. Woodstock, NY: The Overlook Press, 1974).

.........The Book of Five Rings. Translated by Thomas Cleary. Boston, MA: Shambhala, 2005.

Nardi, Thomas J. "Folklore of Tai Chi." Martial Art (Jul. 2003).

Paret, Peter. Makers of Modern Strategy. Edited by Peter Paret. Princeton, NJ: Princeton University Press, 1986.

PBS. Secrets of the Samurai Sword: Way of the Warrior. Nova. http://www.pbs.org/wgbh/nova/samurai/way-nf.html.

Petermann, Stephen with Franck, Loren. "Shatter Your Nightmares." Martial Art (Aug. 2003).

Rand, Christopher C. "Li Ch'uan and Chinese Military Thought." Harvard Journal of Asian Studies, Vol. 39, No. 1 (Jun. 1979).

Rogers, David. "No-Nonsense Kung-Fu." Inside Kung-Fu. http://www.insidekung-fu.com.

Rosenbaum, Michael. Kata and the Transmission of Knowledge in Traditional Martial Arts. Boston, MA: YMAA Publication Center, 2004.

Rothenberg, G. E. *Makers of Modern Strategy*. Edited by Peter Paret. Princeton, NJ: Princeton University Press, 1986.

Rovere, Dennis. *The Xingyi Quan of the Chinese Army*. Translated by Chow Hon Huen. Berkeley, California: Blue Snake Books, 2008.

Ryor, Kathleen. *Military Culture in Imperial China*. Edited by Nicola Di Cosmo. Cambridge, MA: Harvard University Press, 2009.

Saha, Subrata. *China's Grand Strategy: From Confucius to Contemporary*. U.S. Army War College.

Sawyer, Ralph D. *One Hundred Unorthodox Strategies: Battle and Tactics of Chinese Warfare*. Boulder, CO: Westview Press, 1996.

Sawyer, Ralph and Sawyer, Mei-chün. *The Seven Military Classics of Ancient China including The Art of War*. Boulder, CO: Westview Press, 1993.

Scobell, Andrew. *China's Use of Military Force: Beyond the Great Wall and the Long March*. New York, NY: Cambridge University Press, 2003.

Starkey, Armstrong. "Paoli to Stony Point: Military Ethics and Weaponry during the American Revolution." *The Journal of Military History*, Vol. 58, No. 1 (Jan. 1994).

Strachan, Hew. *Clausewitz's On War*. New York, NY: Atlantic Monthly Press, 2007.

Strachan, Hew and Herberg-Rothe, Andreas. Editors. *Clausewitz in the Twenty-First Century*. New York, NY: Oxford University Press, 2007.

Suarez, Gabriel. "Musashi for the 21st Century." *Black Belt* (May 2004).

Sun Tzu. *The Art of War*. Translated by Lionel Giles. New York, NY: Barnes and Nobles Classics, 2003.

.........*The Art of War*. Translated by Thomas Cleary. Boston, MA: Shambhala Publications, 1988.

Swope, Ken. *Continuing Strategic Traditions & Creating Strategic Cultures*. Lecture. Norwich University, VT, 2006.

Tao Hanzhang. *Sun Tzu's Art of War: The Modern Chinese Interpretation*. Translated by Yuan Shibing. New York, NY: Sterling Innovation, 2006.

Tegner, Bruce. *Savate: French Foot & Fist Fighting*. Ventura, CA: Thor Publishing Company, 1983.

Tetsuro Sumida, Jon. *Decoding Clausewitz: A New Approach to On War*. Lawrence, KS: University Press of Kansas, 2008.

Thucydides. *The Peloponnesian War*. New York, NY: E. P. Dutton, 1910.

.........*The Peloponnesian War: The Complete Hobbes Translation, with notes and introduction by David Grene*. Chicago, IL: University of Chicago Press, 1989.

Torres, J. "Continuous Fist Fighting." Interview with Sid Campbell. *Black Belt* (May 2004).

United States Marine Corps. *Warfighting*, 1989. Based on Clausewitz's *On War*.

Vargo, Keith. "Way of the Warrior: Martial Art or Martial Science." *Black Belt* (Feb. 2003).

........."Way of the Warrior: Truth Seekers." *Black Belt* (May 2004).

Ven, Hans van de. *Warfare in Chinese History*. Boston, MA: Brill Academic Publishing, 2000.

Wagner, Jim. "The Fast-Food Menu Concept." *Black Belt* (Aug. 2005).

Waldron, Arthur. "Sun Tzu." *The Reader's Companion to Military History*. Edited by Robert Cowley & Geoffrey Parker. New York, NY: Houghton Mifflin Company, 1996.

Waley-Cohen, Joanna. *Military Culture in Imperial China*. Edited by Nicola Di Cosmo. Cambridge, MA: Harvard University Press, 2009.

Weber, Tamas. "Budo on the Battlefield." Interview by Jose Fraguas. *Martial Arts & Combat Sports* (Jun. 2002).

Weiss, Al and Weiss, David. *The Official History of Karate in America: The Golden Age: 1968-1986*. Los Angeles, CA: Pro-Action Publishing, 1997.

Wilson, Terry L. "Shock & Awe." *Martial Art* (Sep. 2003).

Wiltse, Lucas. "Good Kung Fu: Meeting Wing Chun Master Lo Man Kam." *Travel in Taiwan* (Jul./Aug. 2010).

Wolf, Tony. "A System Which He Termed Bartitsu." *Journal of Manly Arts: European and Colonial Combatives, 1776-1914* (May 2006).

Xue Fei. "Know Your Major: Sanda." *Global Times* (Dec. 29, 2009).

Yamamoto Tsunetomo. *Hagakure: The Book of the Samurai*. Translated by William Scott Wilson. New York, NY: Kodansha, 1983.

Zhang Yun. *The Art of Chinese Swordsmanship*. Boston, MA: Weatherhill, 1998.

Zhuge Liang. *The Way of the General*, translated by Thomas Cleary. http://kongming.net/novel/writings/wotg/.